# "BUT HE DOESN'T KNOW THE TERRITORY"

Also by Meredith Willson
Published by the University of Minnesota Press

*And There I Stood with My Piccolo*

*Meredith Willson*

# "BUT HE DOESN'T KNOW THE TERRITORY"

The Story behind *Meredith Willson's*
*The Music Man*

*Broadway Edition*

Foreword by Michael Feinstein

University of Minnesota Press
Minneapolis | London

Lyrics from *The Music Man*, including "Rock Island Rock," "My White Knight," "Ya Got Trouble," and "Seventy-Six Trombones," copyright 1957 by Frank Music Corporation. Reprinted by permission of the copyright proprietor, which reserves all rights.

Originally published in 1959 by G. P. Putnam's Sons
First University of Minnesota Press edition, 2009
Second University of Minnesota Press edition, 2020
Copyright 1959 by Meredith Willson
Copyright renewed 1987 by Rosemary Willson
Foreword to the Second University of Minnesota Press edition copyright 2020 by Michael Feinstein

Published by the University of Minnesota Press
111 Third Avenue South, Suite 290
Minneapolis, MN 55401-2520
http://www.upress.umn.edu

LIBRARY OF CONGRESS CATALOGING-IN-PUBLICATION DATA
Willson, Meredith, 1902–1984, author. | Feinstein, Michael, writer of
    foreword.
"But he doesn't know the territory" : the story behind *Meredith Willson's
    The Music Man* / Meredith Willson ; foreword by Michael Feinstein.
Broadway edition. | Minneapolis : University of Minnesota Press, 2020.
Identifiers: LCCN 2020022318 | ISBN 978-1-5179-1047-1 (pb) |
    ISBN 978-1-4529-6501-7 (ebook)
Subjects: LCSH: Willson, Meredith, 1902–1984. | Composers—United
    States—Biography. | Willson, Meredith, 1902–1984. Music man.
Classification: LCC ML410.W714 A3 2020 | DDC 792.6/42—dc23
LC record available at https://lccn.loc.gov/2020022318

Printed in the United States of America on acid-free paper

The University of Minnesota is an equal-opportunity educator and employer.

28 27 26 25 24 23 22 21 20     10 9 8 7 6 5 4 3 2 1

*To my Rini*

MICHAEL FEINSTEIN

# Foreword to the Broadway Edition

How did he do it? How did a man who had never written a Broadway musical before end up writing the book, music, and lyrics for one of the most enduring classics of all time, challenging the status quo and confounding the claque of naysayers when he aced the assignment? The answer lies herein. It's a heroic story and one that the subject in question, Meredith Willson, tells with the same light, charming, and deft touch that permeates his enduring masterwork (and subject of this tome), *The Music Man.*

Even if you're from Mars and have never heard of *The Music Man,* this book will entertain and educate you because it:

- is a darn good read
- paints a likeable portrait of its protagonist for

whom you will feel empathy, even though you may know nothing about the world of musical theater

- gives (with humility) a lesson in perseverance and self-reliance

- will make you long for the "old days" even if you're twelve; even if you hate the "old days"; even if the "old days" never existed

- will make you laugh

- will help you feel more creative than you were before you picked it up

- is timeless

- is suspenseful as it moves toward its climax

- does not take itself too seriously and puts everything in perspective

- is one of the best documented chronicles illustrating the collaborative process of birthing a musical.

Let's take a closer look at the last point.

There are hundreds of books out there where we can find out anything we might desire to know about the art and craft of writing and producing a Broadway musical. Every conceivable angle has been covered and recounted and shared, and there are many gems among their legions where one can learn the "ropes." Alongside all these corporeal tomes, the internet has expanded the back stories of Broadway to infinity. So you might say that there's enough on the subject.

[ viii

But none of them is like this one. This is the first-person perspective of a deeply canny and meticulous chronicler who managed to preserve the creative process as if it were spontaneously happening, catching the mundane moments and details that illuminate and humanize the story. The moment-to-moment ups and downs, ins and outs, and subtly shifting creative process that career forward like a roller coaster all somehow make sense, and those details illustrate in most vivid terms what it feels like to solve a puzzle for which you're not certain you have all the pieces.

It took an unusual soul to manifest a musical as inevitable and personal as *The Music Man*, and indeed its author was mightily eclectic, though it wasn't until his Broadway triumph that his contemporaries came to see him for all that he was. Robert Reiniger Meredith Willson was a man of unquestionable musical talent, amply demonstrated in the years preceding his bold and rather belated entry into musical theater. He didn't start working on the show until he was fifty, and then famously spent seven years immersed in that bumpy journey.

As a younger man during the 1920s and 1930s, Willson had worked in many different areas of music and was part of a new American breed of musician not confined to one type or genre. This was partly due to his childhood rearing in the heartland of Mason City, Iowa, and his fervent involvement with marching bands, salon music, and popular songs, alongside classical training on the flute. Later he worked with John Philip Sousa, Toscanini, and the New York Philharmonic, and for a relatively brief period wrote notable film music, which was distinguished by two Academy Award nominations. He became the all-important director of music for NBC radio on the West Coast and programmed popular music for NBC radio while writing two symphonies and other orchestral works. Starting in the late 1930s he established himself not only as an orchestra leader but as a personality, particularly on the MGM *Good News* shows where he participated in sketches and told jokes, affecting a sometimes wacky persona that the audiences loved. Through working on radio, he learned much about musical storytelling and had the luxury of a decades-long apprenticeship in a field that allowed him to experiment with ideas that later were incorporated into *The Music Man,* such as "The Talking People," an a cappella group of nonsinging voices all speaking in unison. This combination of varied musical ability along with show business experience provided Willson the seminal DNA to write his first Broadway show.

Even though I never met him, I have always felt a personal connection to Willson and his music from the first time I heard *The Music Man.* When his widow Rosemary came to one of my shows and introduced herself, I was deeply thrilled, and we eventually became close friends. She was a kind, gentle, and self-effacing person who fiercely protected her husband's legacy, always being mindful of fulfilling his wishes and doing the right thing. They were married in 1968, after the death of his beloved Rini, and Rosemary (who had been his proper and businesslike secretary for years) was genuinely shocked when he asked her on a date. She first came to know the man

[ x

professionally and then later intimately, giving her a special loving bond to him and never getting over the wonder of having become his wife.

The first time I visited their home I was both excited and moved to see where he had lived and created so much remarkable work. The year was 2004 and Meredith had been gone for twenty years, yet it still felt as if at any moment he might walk into the room and add a flourish to the manuscript still sitting upon the piano. When Rosemary allowed me to go through his papers and musical effects, I was able to physically peruse what he wrote about in this book: the endless drafts, cut songs, demo recordings, and innumerable ephemera relating to the show, as the piles of stuff demonstrated the years of ups, downs, stops, and starts. There were odd songs light years away from the story as we know it, and among them was the original demo recording for the tune that later became "The Wells Fargo Wagon" when the show was still titled *The Silver Chalice*. That first version was called "The Blue Ridge Mountains of North Car'line," and although it is a perfectly charming song, when the Wells Fargo words were appended to the tune, magic was born. Suddenly music that had seemed mundane when wedded to the "North Car'line" idea came to life with a locomotion that created theater magic. Wow! How long, I wondered, did it take Meredith to figure it out and make that transition? So many questions came with every scrap of paper.

After Rosemary's passing, the charitable foundation that she had formed that is now known as The Music Man Foundation carefully divided and thematically donated

Meredith's papers to three institutions, among them one I helped to found called The Great American Songbook Foundation. That is where you can find his working materials for this classic show safely sequestered and preserved for visitors and scholars wishing to study them.

As you will learn from his writing, Meredith penned this musical as a love letter to his home state and the people who were part of it. *The Music Man* is not an international show compared to other Broadway blockbusters; while it is performed in other countries, most of the interest is domestic. I suspect that Meredith Willson would be fine with that, for he always went against convention and followed his stubborn heart.

Look what it got him.

# "BUT HE DOESN'T KNOW THE TERRITORY"

# *Foreword*

I almost never read a Foreword, myself. Unless it is very short. I've noticed the same thing about a lot of other people. Once they do finish a Foreword though, I've also noticed the chances are fair that they will continue for a ways. Even if what follows happens to be:

# Foreword Two

Words holler at me. I mean they are more sound than symbol. So I'd like to say that I am not illiterate to the point indicated by the way I misuse, in the following account, some of the simplest words in the dictionary. The reason is that I can't always bring myself to put down the word "sit," for instance, when I know good and well I say "set," more than half the time. Also my brother and I and the rest of the people from home never say just "over," it's always "overt." "Overt" the store, "overt" your house, "overt" our house. Most everybody at home says "prob'ly," too; some people I know back home with three, four diplomas say things like "they come in and set down." And we always say "of" when we mean "have" like "I could never of done it." Anyway, I like my speech to look in some degree like it sounds. That's no more than just being ordinarily truthful. I do like some of the longer words, too, if they rattle pleasantly around in the ear, which is the way I would like to sound when I'm talking, if I had time to think them out, as you do once in a while when you're writing.

During the years I was working on this musical, Rini and I went to a good many Broadway shows. Sitting there we would automatically try to imagine that the orchestra in the pit was playing *The Music Man* overture on opening night. This practice was *mas*ochistic—*mas*ochistic—*mas*ochistic—ah, words. How's that for a steam locomotive—a 1912 6-8 wheeler double-heading through the Royal Gorge—*mas*ochistic!—*mas*ochistic!—*mas*ochistic!—*mas*ochistic! When I was a kid we'd set around and repeat words over and over just for the heck of it, any words at all, till they got so they were just crazy sounds that didn't have any meaning any more—yet, yet, yet, yet, yet, yet, yet, yet, yet, sugar, sugar, sugar, sugar, shu-gar, shu-gar, shu—gar, shu-u-u-gar.

Trying to visualize the orchestra in the different Broadway theatres playing *The Music Man* opening-night overture was indeed masochistic because it made my stomach turn over and my heart bam up into my throat. Now I'm not going to set here and pretend I haven't had my share of apprehension and thrill through the years. The childhood ones, of course, were the big ones. There was this red and golden-brown September morning, for instance, standing in front of the fortuneteller tent at the Cerro Gordo County Fair. Having run some errands for my Uncle O., I was about to get my spending money for the day. Well he gave me a silver dollar. The first dollar I ever had.

Or the time Christmas Eve at the church when they had the program in the main part instead of the lecture room and Mr. Rau had his stereoptican all heated up—there in

[ 6

the balcony over the clock, and just at the climax of showing his Christmas slides when everybody knew the next
thing would be the Star of Bethlehem slide Mr. Rau had
made himself and which he showed all over the church
ceiling every year moving it all around to make it look
realistic instead of just on the sheet down on the platform,
and we knew he always needed someone to help him tip
the big stereoptican back, to shine the star around that
way, and he called out: "Will Cedric Willson please come
to the balcony?" Cedric is my brother;

or when Mr. Keeler, Mason City's famous musician who
studied in Boston, said I was good enough on the flute to
play a piece for the Kiwanis Club at the Cerro Gordo Hotel
Wednesday noon;

or later that same summer when I was not only asked
to play flute and piccolo in the Mason City Municipal Band
but I was to be permitted to sort the music in the high
school basement and carry it to and from the Bandstand
every night—and twice on Sundays;

or when the last night that summer the leader of that
band, Mr. James Fulton, offered me a drink of dandelion
wine he made himself;

or when Willow Creek became a River. When my mother
was a young lady she went to the Armour Institute in
Chicago, then married my father and went to Iowa and
outside of two trips to Aunt Lida's in Topeka and one trip
to Charles City 28 miles east on the Milwaukee to Uncle
Ed's funeral, Mama never left Mason City till the day she
died. Mama was always preoccupied with nice things—like
never call your mother or even any other lady "she." Keep

mentioning their name, no matter how many times. Mama worried about being nice to animals, too—Mama ran out in front several times a day to urge a man going by to unhook the checkrein on his horse, and if he didn't Mama sent the first boy to come by on a bicycle flying off to Mr. Nutting of the Humane Society. And the boys always went, they loved Mama because she always treated them like individuals. Mama also worried about the people at the post office having things made unnecessarily awkward for them, like for example to her dying day Mama was convinced that letters are addressed backwards. "The last thing," Mama said, "that the post office people care about is the name of the person. The first thing they need to know is the country, then the state, and so on." Like the correct way to address the envelope is as follows:

> U.S.A.
> Iowa
> Mason City
> 324 South Superior Street
> Rosalie Willson

And Mama liked nice-sounding words. Instead of ordinary ones like "Creek." So Mama set about a good many years ago to prove that Willow Creek—a noble enough stream running beneath the South Superior Street bridge five houses south of our house—was not a Creek at all but a River. Lime Creek on the other side of town was similarly unsatisfactory to Mama and her efforts to provide these streams with official dignity embraced a lot of research and bales of correspondence proving among other things during the process why Mason City was settled where it was settled: Indians always located their villages at the confluence of two rivers—not creeks, *rivers*—thus, according to their belief, insuring peace and fertility. Well sir, the Indian camp which became a village which became Owens Grove which became Shiboleth which became Mason Grove which became Masonville which became Mason City was settled by Indians "at the confluence of two Rivers," said Mama. "Mason City is a River City, not a Creek City, and I am not at all sure that our Willow River does not have its source in the Winnebago." And my mother did finally and officially prove this to be so.

Now I'm not belittling those thrills, nor for that matter, the later ones after I grew up and left home—playing the piccolo with Sousa; and the flute with Toscanini; there was also my first published composition—*you can't hardly top that,* except maybe the first performance of it, even if it was only by a dance band because you knew the banjo player.

But what I'm saying is, and I'm sorry to be so round about—although that is one of the most generally accepted Iowa characteristics—you can take *all* the rolly-coaster rides of a fairly long and very happy career and you can roll them all together and multiply them by ten and triple-plate them with platinum-covered uranium in spades, and you have got nothing compared to sitting there in a Broadway theatre with a first-night audience, and your show back there behind that curtain and your company praying for you as you are praying for them, and your Rini sitting there beside you in the furthest two seats overt the side

9 ]

under the box nearest the exit, plenty places to hide, easy to duck out fast, tightly holding her cold hand with its wet palm in your cold hand with its wet palm, as the lights dim down and out—as suddenly the show curtain gets hit with a million candle power—as now, now, now, at long, long last, with you knowing positively it could never happen, the conductor raises his baton.

The number of things that can go through your mind in a half a split second reaches off into the countless, people say; adding up to a whole lifetime. As when you're drowning; or falling from a building; or waiting for the blade of a guillotine; or the downbeat of a baton.

*The Music Man* produced by Kermit Bloomgarden with Herbert Greene in association with Frank Productions, Inc., directed by Morton Da Costa, opened at the Majestic Theatre, New York City on December 19, 1957 with the following cast:

## CAST

*(In order of appearance)*

TRAVELLING SALESMEN .............. *Russell Goodwin, Hal Norman, Robert Howard, James Gannon, Robert Lenn, Vernon Lusby, Robert Evans*

CHARLIE COWELL ........................ *Paul Reed*
CONDUCTOR ........................... *Carl Nicholas*
HAROLD HILL ........................ *Robert Preston*
MAYOR SHINN ......................... *David Burns*
EWART DUNLOP .................. *Al Shea* ⎫
OLIVER HIX ................. *Wayne Ward* ⎬ THE
JACEY SQUIRES ............... *Vern Reed* ⎥ BUFFALO
OLIN BRITT ............. *Bill Spangenberg* ⎭ BILLS
MARCELLUS WASHBURN ............. *Iggie Wolfington*
TOMMY DJILAS ........................ *Danny Carroll*
MARIAN PAROO ....................... *Barbara Cook*
MRS. PAROO ............................ *Pert Kelton*
AMARYLLIS ............................ *Marilyn Siegel*
WINTHROP PAROO ..................... *Eddie Hodges*
EULALIE MACKECKNIE SHINN ........ *Helen Raymond*
ZANEETA SHINN ....................... *Dusty Worrall*
GRACIE SHINN ........................ *Barbara Travis*

11 ]

ALMA HIX ................................. *Adnia Rice*
MAUD DUNLOP ........................ *Elaine Swann*
ETHEL TOFFELMIER ................... *Peggy Mondo*
MRS. SQUIRES .......................... *Martha Flynn*
CONSTABLE LOCKE ................... *Carl Nicholas*

RIVER CITY TOWNSPEOPLE AND KIDS

Pamela Abbott, Babs Delmore, Martha Flynn, Janet Hayes, Peggy Mondo, Barbara Williams, Elaine Swann, Marie Santella, Marlys Watters, James Gannon, Russell Goodwin, Robert Howard, Peter Leeds, Robert Lenn, Hal Norman, Carl Nicholas, Joan Bowman, Alice Clift, Nancy Davis, Penny Ann Green, Lynda Lynch, Jacqueline Maria, Marilyn Poudrier, Pat Mariano, Elisabeth Buda, Babs Warden, Tom Panko, Ronn Cummins, Robert Evans, Vernon Lusby, Gary Menteer, John Sharpe, Roy Wilson, Gerald Teijelo, Bob Mariano, Vernon Wendorf.

UNDERSTUDIES

Harold Hill—Larry Douglas; Marian Paroo—Marlys Watters; Mayor Shinn—Paul Reed; Mrs. Paroo—Adnia Rice; Marcellus Washburn—Paul Reed; Charlie Cowell—Hal Norman; Tommy Djilas—John Sharpe; Zaneeta Shinn—Lynda Lynch; Ewart Dunlop—Robert Lenn; Oliver Hix—Russell Goodwin; Jacey Squires—Art Rubin; Olin Britt—Robert Howard; Winthrop Paroo—Bob Mariano; Eulalie Mackecknie Shinn—Adnia Rice; Alma Hix, Maud Dunlop, Ethel Toffelmier—Martha Flynn; Gracie Shinn—Pat Mariano; Amaryllis—Barbara Travis.

Choreography by Onna White
Settings and Lighting by Howard Bay
Costumes by Raoul Pene Du Bois
Musical Direction and Vocal Arrangements by Herbert Greene
Orchestration by Don Walker and Sidney Fine
Dance Arrangements by Laurence Rosenthal
[ 12

## National Company

*The Music Man* produced by Kermit Bloomgarden with Herbert Greene in association with Frank Productions, Inc., directed by Morton Da Costa and with musical direction by Michel Perriere, opened at the Philharmonic Auditorium, Los Angeles on August 18, 1958 with the following cast:

### CAST
*(In order of appearance)*

TRAVELLING SALESMEN ............... *Lewis Bolyard, Walter Kelvin, Lou Polacek, Richard Fredricks, Rudy Jenkins, Jimy Weiss, Chas. Karel*

CHARLIE COWELL ....................... *Harry Hickox*
CONDUCTOR ............................. *Earl George*
HAROLD HILL ........................... *Forrest Tucker*
MAYOR SHINN ............................ *Cliff Hall*
EWART DUNLOP ............ *Byron Mellberg* } THE FRISCO FOUR
OLIVER HIX .................... *James Ingram* } THE FRISCO FOUR
JACEY SQUIRES .................. *Jay F. Smith* } THE FRISCO FOUR
OLIN BRITT ...................... *Allan Louw* } THE FRISCO FOUR
MARCELLUS WASHBURN .............. *Benny Baker*
TOMMY DJILAS .......................... *Robert Piper*
MARIAN PAROO ......................... *Joan Weldon*
MRS. PAROO ........................ *Lucie Lancaster*
AMARYLLIS ................................ *Kay Cole*
WINTHROP PAROO ....................... *Lynn Potter*

EULALIE MACKECKNIE SHINN .......... *Carol Veazie*
ZANEETA SHINN ...................... *Susan Luckey*
GRACIE SHINN ........................... *Jan Tanzy*
ALMA HIX .............................. *Jean Bruno*
MAUD DUNLOP ................. *Mary Alice Wunderle*
ETHEL TOFFELMIER .................... *Lu Leonard*
MRS. SQUIRES ...................... *Marceline Decker*
CONSTABLE LOCKE ..................... *Earl George*

RIVER CITY TOWNSPEOPLE AND KIDS

Micki Barton, Peggy Brooks, Joan Duncan, Marilyn Fisk, Dianne La Mond, Mary Mason, Ann Sparkman, Barbara Beck, James E. Barron, Lee Capo, Rudy Jenkins, Jim McArdle, Bert Michaels, Will Nagel, Jimy Weiss, Chad Thompson, Dianne Barton, Ceil Delly, Marceline Decker, Lu Leonard, Donna Linnard, Terry Marone, Jean Bruno, Patricia Sickelsmith, Lewis Bolyard, Robert Cosden, Luther Durham, Charles Karel, Lou Polacek, Richard Fredricks.

UNDERSTUDIES

Harold Hill—Harry Hickox; Marian Paroo—Dianne Barton; Mayor Shinn—Earl George; Mrs. Paroo—Mary Alice Wunderle; Marcellus Washburn—Earl George; Charlie Cowell—Earl George; Tommy Djilas—Bert Michaels; Zaneeta Shinn—Mary Mason; Ewart Dunlop—Lou Polacek; Oliver Hix—Richard Fredricks; Jacey Squires—Lou Polacek; Olin Britt—Walter Kelvin; Winthrop Paroo—Jeffery Allan; Eulalie Mackecknie Shinn—Jean Bruno; Alma Hix, Maud Dunlop, Ethel Toffelmier —Marceline Decker; Amaryllis—Jan Tanzy.

[ 14

# Chapter One

It was in 1951 when the most successful team of producers of Broadway musical comedies to date telephoned me about writing a show for them. Their names were Ernie Martin and Cy Feuer. They said, "Mere, we think you could write a musical comedy."

And I say, "What about?"

And they says, "About your Iowa boyhood, with the common touch you have occasionally demonstrated as in this song you recently wrote for Tallulah's radio program 'May the Good Lord Bless and Keep You.'"

Ernie says, "You also had the common touch in your book a few years back. Something about There You Stood with Your Piccolo."

"'*And* There I Stood with My Piccolo,'" I says, surprised and flattered but trying not to sound it. "I'll have to think about it." Actually Rini had suggested I write a musical comedy 6,741 times before, pointing out that along with the music I had written a lot of lyrics through the years, and a couple books—why shouldn't I combine forces with myself in a musical comedy? Being Iowa-stubborn I had merely bōwed my neck (as in bow-and-arrow and as in neck-bowed Hawkeye) and resisted the whole idea in the typical posture of irrefragability that is the normal Iowa response to any suggestion of any nature whatsoever. It was therefore easy and natural for me to reassume this attitude for Feuer and Martin as well as for Frank Loesser, my close friend of a considerable number of years standing, who had made a similar suggestion around that same time.

So, one day, without giving the matter too much thought, I wrote ACT ONE, SCENE ONE on the empty paper, not, of course, to show these people that I could write a musical comedy but to show them I could not. And for the next six years I was way out in front.

I looked at those fatal four words on the paper for some little time, that first day. ACT ONE, SCENE ONE. I look at them now. They seem harmless enough just anywhere along the page like this. But up at the top of an empty piece of paper they commit you, in some horrible way, like your name was Faust and you just signed a contract with the Devil. Sure, it's only you, but you're committed, just the same. You're stuck with yourself.

ACT ONE, SCENE ONE. So far so good. The *fifth* word was the sticker, though. Couldn't locate that fifth word. So I just sat there. Quite some time went by. Three years in fact. Oh no, I got up from the typewriter. I'm not that industrious. Besides I had to keep the store open, which gave me considerable pause, what with my old profession in radio and TV dwindling away from me and my new profession as playwright refusing to progress beyond the first four words. I had one foot in a departing boat and the other on a receding dock, as you could say. I did get some words down, though, even if they weren't consecutive to Act One, Scene One. It happened while I was sitting there at the typewriter on the defensive one day, thinking about those who were, through no effort of their own, born with the ability to calmly hitch up their pants, write ACT ONE, SCENE ONE and proceed with a play. And those who weren't. I remembered that the composer Von Weber was a dead-center man who couldn't compose for sour apples until he first hit a D and an F-sharp on the piano. He'd listen to those vibrations for a while and all of a sudden he was a ball of fire. I tried D and F-sharp on the piano myself. Nothing. Of course not, I thought. You prime music with music. Words you got to prime with words. Maybe I will just start out with a page or two of the first things that come into my head, get oiled up with a couple hundred words—at least break the stillness of the room. Then maybe I could sneak back to Act One, Scene One without noticing. It's worth a try, I thought. Otherwise I might set here forever looking at the keys, trying to pick out one to punch. I glanced absently up at a picture of some guys I have framed up over the desk there in my music room. Being nearsighted I was only able to pick out the one blond kid with the white face.

What the heck was his name again? All of a sudden I was typing. *Tank,* I wrote. That was the kid's name.

Alvin Tank. He was the oldest. He's holding an alto in a picture I have framed up over the desk in my music room. It is a picture of Mason City's first High School Band, back in 1912. One piccolo (me), two clarinets, two cornets, one euphonium, one tuba, one snare drum, one bass drum, one trombone and Alvin Tank with this alto. One of the first things I learned when I became a professional musician was that there is nothing as completely futile as one alto. An alto was of course called a peck horn in my day because it was never used on the tune—only on the afterbeats: "mm *peck,* mm *peck,* mm *peck-a- peck-peck.*" And afterbeats should always be two-ply, as you could say, in order to provide the necessary harmony. A half-a-peck is worse than no peck at all. So one alto was pretty futile even though Alvin Tank was the oldest.

In this picture I have framed up over my desk we are all grimly posed in the non-smiling tradition of group picture-taking of those days. Anybody caught smiling, or even thinking, was a sissy. The amazing thing was that there was no leader in the picture. Remembering back, it suddenly comes to me we didn't *have* any leader! Herr Koch, our German teacher, was musical but he played a violin—out of place in a band. He was, therefore, only the leader of the orchestra, made up mostly of seniors, including girls in their long dresses which included Marion Maguire. She played the cello parts on her brother's euphonium sitting there in her long dress. Which is why we could rehearse only every other Tuesday night—we had to alternate with the orchestra so Mickey, Marion's brother, could use the euphonium for a euphonium in the band when Marion wasn't using it for a cello in the orchestra. Actually it was very much in character for a girl in innocent Iowa, stop to think about it, to play the cello part on an instrument that you held in your lap instead of between your knees. Both the orchestra and the band were purely voluntary and came into existence just for Tuesday evening recreation because some of us had found out we were musical and Tuesday was a good available night. Like on Monday nights, you'd listen to Papa and Sister playing cribbage. ("Fifteen-two, fifteen-four, fifteen-six, and a pair is eight"—How I could've listened to that strange formula every Monday night throughout my entire childhood and never had the curiosity to find out why they kept saying it strikes me as being kind of alarming as I look back.) Wednesday night was choir practice, of course. We used to add "under the bed" to the different hymn titles—I don't mean out loud, I mean there in the hymnbook, not with pencil but pricking the letters in with a pin, which for some reason seemed to us to be less of a mutilation of God's property than pencil. Christian Endeavor was Thursday night unless you were a Methodist. They had the same thing over there but they called it Epworth League. Friday night, the Star Theatre showed the current installment of Marguerite Snow in *The Million-Dollar Mystery*. Or *The Trey of Diamonds*. Saturday night there was usually some place to go with your mother like an evening of some kind at the library. The library always looked like such a completely different place in the evening. I didn't care for it. Other times you'd go downt the church, if it was Hyperian or Redpath night, to see Blind Boone play the piano, or Bohumir Kryl with his daughters and his cornet in his uniform with all his medals. And of course we went to regular church Sunday night, for the third time that day, counting Sunday school. That left every other Tuesday night for band practice.

I don't think any of us in the band would ever have believed it if we had been told that the day would come when you'd rehearse your high school band in the daytime in a special music building connected with the school —the Wagner-Mozart Building—and actually get credits for it like for Current Events or Physics. And I had sure forgotten we didn't have any leader. Who in the world started us off? Alvin Tank was the oldest, but he couldn't possibly have started us off holding a peck horn, which is quite a bit different from doing it holding a cornet. All winter we'd meet at the different boys' houses. The program was always the same, though I can't remember our ever performing it any place except in our different houses every other Tuesday night. First "The Crusader Overture," then "Our Director" (a somewhat wistful choice considering we had no director), next "The National Emblem" which we could never really get anywhere with but never gave up working at, and finally the Minuet in G which was the one piece we could always manage to get through somehow without stopping. With or near the ten o'clock striking of the courthouse clock Mrs. Tank, or Mrs.

[ 20

Maguire or Mrs. Kuppinger would find a tactful place to interrupt. "Boys," she'd say, "how about a nice plate of cream?"

The picture must have been taken for the High School Annual my freshman year because I am still in knee pants. Nowadays, of course, the children put on long pants when they enter first grade. I was the youngest and Alvin Tank was the oldest. Whenever I look back through the annuals I can pick out a couple of guys out of every graduating class that turned out to be the kind of people people still change the subject over whenever their name comes up back home. I mean guys who were in jail or should be, or things like that. But none of those guys were any of the guys who showed up every other Tuesday to try to play "The National Emblem" on their own time. Although one day when my Aunt Mae was talking to Mrs. Dr. Smith (Mama always said to give a lady her husband's title if any) Mrs. Dr. Smith said—forgetting Aunt Mae was my aunt—"I hear that Willson boy is traveling with Sousa's Band. Thank goodness *our* children are normal." *Got to get Mama into this show.*

# Chapter Two

Well it seemed that I was oiled up, at least to the extent that I was now ambulating on the paper instead of wearing out the window staring through it. I worried a lot about jokes. Got to have jokes in a musical. My humorous Iowa remembrances were apt to be pretty mild for Broadway—what Georgie Jessel used to affectionately call "Willson's goy fun." The first dirty joke I ever heard was when I was eight—told to me by my older cousin Olie, whose folks had come over for the Fourth of July from Orange City. It was after dark and my brother Cedric and Olie and I were out in the back yard. Standing up against the back fence. I didn't really have to "go" but I wanted to be polite. Cousin Olie, the sophisticate, looked up at the stars that night while we's standing there. "Ever hear about the girl and her first buggy ride with a fella? See, she was scared the horse would do his business while they were driving and embarrass her. So her mother says, 'If that happens just look up at the stars and change the subject.'

So they're out in the country driving slow along the road and sure enough the horse starts doing number one—gallons and gallons, like he's going on forever. So the girl looks up at the stars and says, 'Henry, can you find the Big Dipper?' "

Six more months went by. I hadn't found word number five as such but I had written some thirty priming "essays" about my Iowa boyhood plus twenty songs about the people and the situations therein. Now what? Should I try to peddle this stuff individually? Forget trying to write in play form? Should I? Or shouldn't I? Then one morning the phone entered this cul-de-sac with a ring that almost broke my neck. It was my agent's agent with a big opportunity to fly immediately back to New York and audition for a new TV quiz show called *The Big Surprise* involving a $100,000 jack-pot question. I was told I was practically set to be MC. I kicked away the boat and grabbed for the dock with a crystal-clear conscience. The producer of this new show was also producer of the big hit, *$64,000 Question*, which automatically made his follow-up a guaranteed hit. A guy would have to be out of his mind to turn it down.

Rini and I arrived in New York the next day. My representative met us. "They're pretty happy with you in the MC spot, Meredith," says he. "Your Iowa style will be real offbeat, they think. In fact for the audition, they are doing a complete performance in NBC's Studio 6B with sponsor, agency, contestants, camera and *audience*. That's how *sure* they are." He hit me a gentle roundhouse old-pal-old-keed tap on the chin, and presently I was reading a dummy script over for one of the program's producers. Full of confidence from my representative's pep talk, I kept looking for little places to ad-lib "my Iowa style." The producer interrupted me. "No, no, Meredith, just say 'You're *right!* You're absolutely *right!*' And, Meredith." He took a confidential tone. "Throw yourself forward on the ball of your foot as you say it."

"You're *right!* You're *absolutely right!*" I says.

"Fine," says the producer.

"*Right*, you're *absolutely right!*" I says. "Do you want me to always say that?"

"Oh yes," he says. "Oh yes. Sounds good."

"*Right*," I says and very shortly thereafter we went overt NBC's 6B Studio, which was loaded with audience and glittering with cameras and scenery.

The show opened with shadow effects and electronic music and echo-chamber voices. First a private detective was introduced, psychologically making everything safe and expensive and official. Then an IBM machine, making everything modern and honest. Then I came springing out. Ever see people come springing out? That's a trick you accomplish merely by walking back a few steps into the wings as you hear your cue, then when you come forward again you have a couple extra yards in which to gain momentum before you're visible and you come out onto the gol-darn stage like you were shot out of a bow. So I shot myself on stage, right up to an elaborate space-age podium—chrome and shining—almost overshot it, in fact. And in a very few moments I was crying out "You're *right!*

[ 24

You're *absolutely right!*" to the first contestant, leaning into my delivery as instructed. I cried out like this to two more contestants, even once for a wrong answer. The contestant was so surprised he didn't notice when I evened it up on the next question, calling a ball on him that was right over the old platter. And then. And then. This lady came up, see, and got her winnings up to $50,000.

The $100,000 question was next. It danced on the top half of my card in front of my eyes. The answer to the question was on the bottom half. A very dramatic silence closed in. Leaning forward onto the ball of my right foot, and summoning my loudest clearest tones, I read the lady the answer instead of the question.

I think the company got out of it without paying her the full $100,000 but I never found out for sure.

Rini took all this in from the audience. When the program finished she came up to me and I took her arm. "Very nice, dear," she said calmly looking around. We went across the stage, out into the back, smiling at the different ones, down the steps past the control room through the house and out into the main hall—thence into the elevator and down to the lobby and out to the street. I didn't expect the producer to say good night to us. He didn't. Neither did our fellow actors, the director, the agency men, the sponsors, nor any of the audience. Nor the elevator man. Not even my representative. In fact, we never heard from any of those people ever again.

We were thoughtfully desperate about the whole thing back in the hotel that night. Not resting too well either, we slept in—past lunch. About four o'clock in the afternoon we called room service for some food. Suddenly we burst out laughing. *And* we screamed. *And* we hollered. *And* we roared. *And* we got back on the plane and went home to California.

For a while we just sat around screaming, "You're *right*. You're *absolutely right*" at each other.

There were those other words though—sitting there at the top of that page—ACT ONE, SCENE ONE. I rolled the page into the typewriter. I got out my essays and my twenty songs. In a kind of a quiet rage I continued on, with description at the edge and dialogue in the middle, dividing the material as seemed logical into three acts and seventeen scenes. For what it was worth I had located word number 5.

The story was about a boy's band. It starred a phony band leader and instrument salesman by the name of Harold Hill, actually a con man. As near as I could judge it ran about three hours and forty-five minutes which was pretty near two hours longer than necessary. Or desirable. Meanwhile, since I had last seen Feuer and Martin they had followed their famous production of *Guys and Dolls* with *Can Can,* another big hit, and were already starting on two more: *The Boy Friend* for September and *Silk Stockings* for Christmas. On the theory that if you want something done contact a busy man I wired them HAVE COMBINATION ESSAY, DIALOGUE AND SONG. (Reminds me of the society item in my mother's scrapbook about her wedding: *Prominent among the display of wedding gifts was a lovely combination pickle-dish and ink-stand.* There was a nice comment about the flowers too. *The living room carried out a striking motif being decorated chiefly with syringes.* How Mama shrieked till she cried, laughing at that item. Got to get Mama in this play, I thought almost every time I sat down to the typewriter.) That same day Feuer and Martin answered BRING IT TO NEW YORK IMMEDI-ATELY.

Two nights later Rini and I showed up at Cy Feuer's house in New York fairly well prepared to do all the parts between us and sing all the songs. It was June, I remember.

After the audition we headed back to the hotel. Shoeless morning was just tossing a tentative hat through the door. The taxi we engaged was in automatic adherence to a normalcy we had vacated several hours earlier. Our being ten feet off the ground, it was not only chancy to get in the cab but profligate, considering we could have easily been propelled home by the slip stream of our own head-shaking, characteristically adjunctive to the kind of ad-vanced stages of grinning disbelief in which we found ourselves. We had gone to Cy's that night with quite some lighthearted pride in all those pages and songs, expecting some good-humored reception with maybe some under-standing criticism of the dialogue and possibly some en-thusiasm about the songs. You know the feeling you have when your wife's sick and you cook the dinner? It may smoke a little but if you can get it off the stove onto a plate, you're proud of it. I mean, I'm not any cook but look what *I* did! I was even proud that the thing ran two hours too long. But in our most optimistic moments we didn't expect any such of a reaction as we got. At least I didn't. The subplot, for instance, involved a spastic boy—helpless in a wheel chair—not exactly a character you would normally select for a musical comedy. But Cy and Ernie ate it up—loved it, in fact—along with everything else. Rini, who mixes the language up a little, says smugly, "I knew they'd prance on it the minute they heard it." What they actually said was, "After *The Boy Friend* and *Silk Stockings* our next production will be *The Silver Triangle*." They even made plans to call Josh Logan, the hit director, whose name alone would guarantee the best actors, theatre, choreographer, designer, the best everything, plus a big advance sale at the box office.

"Just don't touch the manuscript," Ernie says to me. Ernest Martin, forty-ish, six feet, dark, worst-dressed man —too hyper-thyroid, no patience for sartorials—slender, except for an eccentric eating revealment in the life-preserver zone, quick-moving, quick to smile—a flashing smile that happens all over his face—disarming, brilliant and effortlessly dominating.

"Put it in a drawer," Cy says. Cyrus Feuer, forty-ish, crew-cut type (Rini says "with a cute bulldog face"), freckled, not dark, not light, five feet nine, takes more time with clothes, rapid-fire thinker but not compulsively either in thought or movement as is Ernie—logical carriage and weight, his grin breaks out easily on his roundish face, also disarming, brilliant and effortlessly dominating.

"At least till after *Silk Stockings* has opened in December," says Ernie.

"The score is great," Cy says.

"All you got to do is shift around the plot and the sub-plot."

"And prune it down."

They both talk a mile a minute, and always in short alternating bursts.

ERNIE: "Of course we gotta change the title."

CY: *"The Silver Triangle* sounds like an Ibsen satire."

"About somebody's middle-aged mistress."

"At the Cherry Lane."

"Need a real Broadway title for a musical."

"You know a Broadway title when you hear it."

"And that ain't it."

"Gotta watch that spastic boy, Mere."

E: "He's news, wonderful news, but he'll steal every scene."

C: "Main thing is to prune him down."

"And shift the accent to the love story."

"Harold Hill is great."

"Larcenous guys like that are always great."

"Sky Masterson."

"What's-his-name Ravenel."

"Jimmy Valentine."

"And what a racket."

"Band instruments, yet!"

They are both projectors, you know. You could hear this dialogue all the way downt the corner—they always talked at the absolute maximum holler-power of their voices. The more they talked the more they found to say. When they really got rolling—well, who do you like for glib—I don't mean glib at all, I mean coherent—Churchill? Clemenceau?

John Daly? Vincent Price in an art gallery? Wrap them all up and you're about halfway to the effect produced by Feuer and Martin. And somehow they never step on each other. It's all like it was rehearsed.

Anyway, everything was peachy-creamy about that night including Cy's wife who does very little yessing about the house and who loved the show on her own, lighting up at all the right places. Her springtime smile came up to Cy's wishbone and her name, "Posy," was the cherry on the soda, the second time in my life I'd ever run across it; the first time was reading over a very flowery love letter up in our Mason City attic from Papa to Mama on the occasion of Mama graduating from Armour Institute. *My adored Posy* it began.

So Rini and I floated home to the hotel in the early morning with our grinnings and head-shakings. We went to bed but not to sleep. "My gosh!" Rini says suddenly sitting up in the dark. "If they'd liked you on that $100,000 thing, you would never have written *The Silver Triangle!*"

"You're *right*. You're *absolutely right!*" I says. "And to think it's *done*. All except for a little pruning and shifting. And a new title." Couple minutes later. "Wonder what we ought to call it." And there went the sleep for that night.

Two weeks later back in California Cy and Ernie phoned from the Beverly Hills Hotel. Ernie opened, with Cy on the extension.

"Josh Logan was very interested."

"Tied up for a year, though."

"With the *Picnic* movie."

"And a thing called *Bus Stop*."

"Also we got a title."

"Like to try it out on you."

"Are you sitting down?"

"Go ahead," I says, "I'm sitting down."

"Not over the phone, Ernie."

"We'll be right out."

In twenty minutes they drove into our driveway. Cy got out of the car first. He didn't even strike an attitude. He just said, "The Music Man!"

Ernie says, "How do you like it?"

"I like it fine," I says, turning to Rini.

"Me too," she says.

Before putting *The Music Man* away in the drawer, however, we thought we should reveal its existence to Abe Lastfogel, head of William Morris, our chief advisor, and Martin Jurow, head of Mr. Lastfogel's drama department. We located them handling one of those magnitudinous deals at Las Vegas, so that's where we went, and between planes Rini and I put on one more performance—this one at 3 P.M. in the cocktail lounge at The Desert Inn to a very appreciative audience of two.

With the monotonous regularity of two country boys in the shooting gallery Ernie Martin and Cy Feuer knocked down all the ducks—*The Boy Friend* got unanimous rave reviews. Hardly waiting to read their telegrams they plunged into *Silk Stockings* due to open in three months. Next, *The Music Man.*

I was now doing ten minutes on radio every day on

"How to Listen to Longhair Music," trying to make a few friends for Mr. Beethoven amongst the "listeners dear." I was also working on a stronger song than the one I had for Harold Hill's first entrance. The lyric was about seventy-six trombones which was working out okay. I liked the melody too, except it seemed to be as good a waltz as it was a march. The more I tried to do something with this nutty circumstance—or drop it, for that matter—the more baffled I became. Like trying to take off a pair of flypaper pajamas. Taping a couple Beethoven shows ahead, Rini and I finally drove off to Idyllwild, six thousand feet up on top of the San Jacinto mountains about three hours' drive from Los Angeles, a favorite retreat when all else fails. After all, I didn't want to lose a march, I wanted to gain a waltz. We got unpacked and I and my problem had been out on the porch for all of fifteen minutes when I was called to the long-distance phone which was located about five hundred yards up the hill. It never occurred to me to ignore the call and stay where I damn was. We get used to most twentieth-century items very quickly such as garage doors that open by thought control from three blocks down the street. The only arresting aspect left in the 707 four-hour jet flight from Los Angeles to New York is that for the first time in history, window shades in a public vehicle can actually be raised and lowered by the passenger. Heck, a do-it-yourself moon making 166,742 miles an hour off in somebody else's solar system can't command the conversational priority of a box of Italian matches any more. But "long distance!" Ah.

Take the other day overt my neighbor's house. My

neighbor was sitting there in the den talking on the phone as I walked in. My father's generation always had the phone in the entrance hall, attached to the wall and accommodated with the rickety taboret your older brother had made downt the manual training class overt the high school—stained it himself, too, I just happened to think. Well, there was my neighbor sitting in his den involved in this phone conversation, so he waved me on into the living room. And that is where I was standing admiring the view with my back to the door when in came my neighbor's ten- by four-inch chihuahua, a fiend from Hell if ever there was one and believe me there was one and this dog is it and he hates me and everybody like me with a malevolence that materialized right then and there with my back turned, in the form of a completely unprovoked attempted homicide; an attack, the relative speed and fury of which you could only compute by meterizing the nozzle of an acetylene blowtorch. Laceration, and shreds. Those are the only words that occur to me now. Well, maimed. Bushwhacked, and lacerated to shreds, my calves, my pants and my dignity. People in the past may have conceivably been in more pain; possibly even more humiliated, though I yield the point only in the interest of minimizing the fissure I have already opened in this narrative. But never has anybody been more outraged. Bleeding my good blood all over my neighbor's white wall-to-wall carpet (a consolation I was not able to take advantage of at the time) and terrified by the snarling of this vixer (a word I just made up out of viper and vixen), his ugly little fangs, anointed with evil spit and framed with quivering raw-red lips drawn back to the tightest possible extent to leave his white needle-pointed gimlets the freeest possible avenue to my flesh, I clawed my way along the wall to the door of the den where my neighbor was still on the phone. "Frank!" I screamed at him. "The dog! Tetanus, somebody! Quick, Frank! Iodine! Rabies! Lockjaw!" And Frank, raising a self-righteous hand says to me, *"Please, I'm talking long distance!"*

And to get back to the priority clarion that echoed clearly through the mountain fastnesses (what the hell is *that!*) on that beautiful gold, green and blue day amongst the pines of Idyllwild: "Meredith Willson! It's *long distance!*" It happened to be Ernie and Cy—it could just as easily have been a wrong number. Cy says, "Where the heck are you?" as though I had missed an appointment and he was standing on a corner some place.

E: "Why don't you stay home?"

C: "What town are you near?" ("Idyllwild," I says.)

"You're probably up at Idyllwild, that's six thousand feet up."

"Got to have The Vertical Wing to land up there."

"Or a chopper. Cy gets sick in a chopper."

"I do, at that. Reminds me of my summer stock days tilting windmills through Connecticut."

"You didn't play the lead you played Sancho Panza."

"Hey, Mere, isn't there a town at the bottom of those mountains?" ("Banning," I says.)

E: "There's a town named Banning near there I think."

C: "Meet you there in half an hour."

[ 34

"At the Banning Air Port." ("I don't think there is any airport," I says.)

But they had hung up.

Well I must say Rini and I should of felt like idiots standing out there in Banning on a strip of old abandoned concrete, racked and overrun with weeds. But we not only stood there, we peered silently and trustingly up into the sky in the direction of Los Angeles. After while *a speck appeared.* As Moran used to say, "I dreamed of flannel cakes and when I woke up *the blanket was gone.*" Well this red plane landed and taxied right up to where we were standing. Cy and Ernie got out, "Hello Mere," they hollered, one at a time, kissed Rini and asked us over to the highway for a cup of coffee like they just got off the streetcar in front of the drugstore.

Over at the Oak Leaf Café, neither the truck drivers nor the ranch hands nor Rini nor I lifted a fork or a cup all the time we were in there, trying to figure out what Ernie and Cy were talking about. Fresh from the Broadway battleground they were loaded and spraying. Ernie's talking about microcosms and armpit shows. Cy lost me from the moment we sat down, discussing the advisability of a "station-house delivery" among the characters and "the ice in the box office," things I never heard of in my life. Back to Ernie and *mac*rocosms, this time. "Not the same thing as microcosms, you know. Not the same thing at all." Then Cy takes a turn telling about their row with George S. Kaufman, author of the *Silk Stockings* book. Back to Ernie. "Quite a Donnybrook," he says. "Kaufman is now telling people that Ernie Martin is Jed Harris all rolled into one. Ohhh—that's a funny joke. Grade-A Kaufman."

Somewhere along the line Cy ordered chili. Ernie didn't order anything. He doesn't drink and appears to live on soft drinks and canned spaghetti and long black cigars. He goes to the world's great restaurants and orders canned spaghetti and coke, always a little provoked that he can't get sarsaparilla or strawberry pop. Jeepers, he'll come to *your house* for dinner and bring his own canned spaghetti.

I finally concluded that what he and Cy are hollering about in this Oak Leaf Café is that they are more excited than ever about *The Music Man*. So much so that there they were in the Oak Leaf Café in Banning instead of being in New York rehearsing their brand-new show *Silk Stockings* and straightening out their rhubarb with Kaufman.

"Cy wants to direct *Music Man*," Ernie finally narrows it down to, "and"—shattering the bemusement of his face into a hundred-faceted smile—"I'd like to help you lick the book. Is that all right with you?"

Well I was certainly "knocked down for a loop" as Rini says. As soon as I realized they had asked me a question I threw in a yes as fast as I could, not to leave any gaping hole hanging there in the dialogue. The three of us hollered at each other a little longer (I don't know if I mentioned I'm a holler-er too, when I get a chance). We then walked back to the airstrip where Rini and I stood like in a crazy dream watching those two fantastic guys climb into that plane and sputter off down the concrete, waving and grinning as they jiggled up into the wild blue.

The New York opening of *Silk Stockings* was delayed till February 21st. On February 22nd while I'm sitting there in Los Angeles trying to get Ernie on the long-distance phone he walked into our house with the reviews in his hand.

"Nancy and I are taking a house in Malibu for six months," Ernie says. Nancy Guild is Ernie's wife, a combination Botticelli, Renoir and Utrillo—and a highly sensitive actress besides. "You and I can work out there by the ocean every day. Or I'll come here. Or alternate. However you want. Just thought you'd enjoy the reviews," and off he went back to New York. The reviews, of course, were smasheroo.

The first day I showed up in Malibu, I came in through the kitchen door, stumbled over a case each of sarsaparilla and strawberry pop and walked over to Ernie's piano. It was nearly a year since Rini and I had auditioned *The Silver Triangle* back in New York at Cy's house that night.

"Hi," says Ernie, "got something new?"

I says, "Yeah. I got a new song for Harold."

I played him "Seventy-Six Trombones." I didn't think it was the right time to tell him I had also used the same melody as a three-four ballad. Particularly when I didn't know what to do with it yet. Although I was getting an idea. Marian was lonesome and lovelorn underneath her stand-offishness. Wasn't Harold lonesome too, despite his flamboyance and girl-in-every-town behavior? Maybe it would be interesting if these two could subtly convey to the audience this characteristic they had in common by separate renderings of the same song—a march for him, a ballad waltz for her. But for Ernie that day I just rendered the march. He beamed like a quarter to three and lit a cigar at the same time, which would be very difficult for anybody else because he was also talking and drinking strawberry pop. "Gee, Mere, I like it."

Next day Ernie came to our house. We got to working to the extent that the time got away from us, right into the dinner hour, in fact. I gave him a coke and started to make myself a cocktail. When he noticed me get a full bottle of small onions out of the icebox, he walked over and took one. He then ate the whole bottle. Not having any canned spaghetti on him I guess he didn't want to take any chance with Rini's dinner—he knew he liked cocktail onions. They took him to Cedars of Lebanon Hospital at two o'clock that morning. I joined him at ten and we worked along as usual.

A very happy beginning. But before many days were over I realized that what we had to do to my manuscript the coming months could never be described as the shifting and pruning so lightly—even invitingly—touched on that night in Cy's apartment. Not only the story had to be rebuilt from the ground up but all the people in it had to be reshaped—their dimensions emphasized with respect to themselves as well as to each other. I now found out the importance of microcosmic significance, as you could say. I also found out what Cy had meant earlier about the "level" of the show. As I had written it, it was "a play with music." Ernie goes on, "Feuer and Martin don't produce 'plays with music'—we produce musical comedies." (This is the time to say clearly I owe more than a great deal to Cy Feuer's theatrical acumen and to Ernie Martin's brilliance in the musical-comedy field as well as to his erudition in the area of applying playwriting principles thereto.)

I went home about six o'clock in the afternoon, had a quick absent-minded supper and went into the music room, closed the door, looked up at Alvin Tank. Alvin and Mama used to visit out in front of the house whenever Alvin passed by. Also Kilroy. Kilroy was another friend of Mama's. Any kid who passed the house was Mama's friend—there was no Catholic, no Protestant, no Jew to Mama, no black, white, tan, red, yellow, no big, little, rich or poor. They were all just Middle-West kids to Mama, who, Mama always said, ought to be exposed to a little gentleness and gentility—a couple good thoughts, and a few nice things, a book, a picture, a quotation, a poem. And the dang kids listened to her, too, even though her advice was not only about what to read but how to act—things kids don't usually like from adults. Got to get Mama into this show.

I looked at the empty page in the typewriter. ACT ONE, SCENE ONE. I could only think of Sadie Teed, a Scandinavian girl who helped Mama on Saturdays, who got sick one summer eating green peaches. "Oh Mrs. Villson, if I could only püke." Maybe I'd be better off to let Act One, Scene One go for today and try to locate the missing microcosm of Tommy, the juvenile character in the show. That brought me back to Kilroy. Tommy was quite a little like Kilroy. In the Egri book on playwriting Ernie gave me to read, I had read about Ibsen, where, in his search for the true nature of his characters, he pretended to get in a railway carriage with them and then engage them in conversation—hear what they had to say. This didn't seem too practical in Kilroy's case. To tell you the truth, I'd be scared to get in a railway carriage with Kilroy. Kilroy seemed older than even the older kids, but I don't think he was, as I look back. He was smaller than any of the older kids. I think he only seemed older because he didn't go to school. He worked. I think he'd only gone a couple years to the convent, I don't know for sure. I only know I was scared of him playing football the way he came tearing down the school yard packing that ball, hollering about his twenty-six operations. Every time we got up a game after school, sooner or later Kilroy would happen along on his way to supper or maybe doing an errand. There was always something about a kid who worked—it always seemed like he had to show the kids who went to school that he could do something better than they could. So whenever we got up a game after school, sooner or later Kilroy would happen along. And that was the signal for whichever team was getting beat to set up a great hue and clamor claiming Kilroy for their side—improvising loud pretexts based on nothing more reasonable than that they were behind—"You guys are way *ahead!* 'Snot *fair*—'snot *fair*—Kilroy plays with us guys! Come on Kilroy! Kilroy's gotta be on our side!" And Kilroy would throw off his coat and charge in there—already

sputtering about his operations in his high-pitched voice.
"I had twenty-six operations! And I can still run you guys
ragged! Not one a' you guys can stop me! Look at you
guys—bigger'n me, every one a' you guys! And I had
twenty-six operations! All right, let's see you stop me!
Just don't get in my room, you guys! Here comes *Kilroy!*
I'm tellin' ya! *Here comes Kilroy*, 8, 12, 14, 37—" He'd
get behind the center and start yelling hysterical signals
in the accepted way of grammar school football games—
just a string of numbers that never meant anything—like
the catcher in our baseball games always exposed a couple
fingers under his mitt before each pitch which never meant
anything either. Kilroy would keep both his fists closed
while he yelled out the numbers. Then he'd just snap
open his fingers and the center would pass the ball back
and Kilroy would huddle himself into a hibernating cater-
pillar ball and start down the field with his particular kind
of full-steam-ahead gallop. Some of his operations were
on his legs—they didn't unbend all the way, one more so
than the other, which gave him a kind of hop. He always
seemed to be running sideways even though he was coming straight at you. Some of his operations were on his
arms which made him have to "grab" the football instead
of "tuck" it anywhere like under his arm or in his gut.
And some were on his neck, even up to the side of his
mouth, which pulled his head over a little. "Twenty-six
operations, you guys! And I'm getting another one next
week! Come on you big guys! You won't stop *me*—not
with *ten* more operations." I got to thinking of Kilroy here
again just the other day when there was something in the

paper about the record football score of all time—a game where the one team made a touchdown on every play. Kilroy always did that. I mean that record game is what caused me to think of Kilroy just recently. I've thought about Kilroy before; a good many times through the years. Quite a good many times. I bet all the guys have. I know I have.

Ernie and I would go over the Music Man story for hours and hours trying to clarify the level and simplify the thread. When I was alone, after getting hopped up with Iowa reminiscences, I'd eventually knock out another draft. Later, Ernie and I would take it apart, end up hating it, and start telling each other the story again, always trying to tell it in half a dozen lines. If we started out once with "There's this flamboyant con guy, see, who sells band instruments," we must of done it five hundred times.

All during that spring and summer I kept rewriting *The Music Man*. Always thought I was getting closer. I mean I always hoped I was. Anyway, every step you take is important, even if it's in exactly the wrong direction, as happened many times, Ernie told me, in the writing of the show he and Cy were proudest of—*Guys and Dolls*.

One major difficulty was that because I respected Ernie's knowledge so highly, I kept trying to write the show just to please him which not only irritated him but frustrated me. And all the time we were together he talked—like a machine gun. Never did I see him search for a word, never heard him say "Ah—." He'd die of fever before any doctor could ever get a look at his tongue. Along with *The Music Man* specifics, we talked a lot about playwriting generalities that summer. One big agreement and one big difference of opinion come to mind. The big agreement related to the familiar argument: to tell 'em or surprise 'em; should we tell the audience at the beginning that Harold is a con man and let them anticipate seeing the unfolding of what they, therefore, already know? Or should we hide this information and let them discover it gradually, to be surprised at the denouement, along with the actors? In the first drafts I had favored the latter. Ernie convinced me I was wrong one day at Malibu. "Look," he says, "you got the favorite character of all audiences—a lovable rogue. How can that terrific asset be going for you unless you tell the audience he's a phony right at the start?" Of course he was right and I started over. Act One, Scene One.

The big difference of opinion was about the songs. I had developed an abiding conviction through the years that in a musical comedy the musical numbers ought to grow out of the dialogue without interruption or jerkiness. Ernie says, "You mean the music should all be justified? Like Zanuck?" Then he told me Darryl Zanuck once issued a blanket order at 20th Century-Fox that he did not want any music in any musical picture from his studio that was not *justified*. Meaning he never wanted to see a guy walk down the street and burst into song accompanied by any unexplained orchestra. If he bursts into song the accompaniment better, by gosh, come from a *justified* source—like a beggar sitting in a doorway with an accordion, or an organ coming from the open door of a church the guy is passing. I argued that wasn't what I meant at all. I argued that the only concern I had was that the song ought to materialize out of the dialogue, and I didn't care how many unjustified musicians there were doing the accompanying in the orchestra pit so long as the audience wasn't *pushed* into song—and then *dragged* out again into dialogue. And *pushed* and *dragged* all evening long. "In fact I'm dying to make the whole show like one song lyric," I says, "dialogue and all. All in one piece."

"So there won't be any pushing and dragging," Ernie says. "Write the show like a lyric, huh. Like a dang poem. Like T. S. Eliot and Christopher Fry. What'll you use for an audience?"

"I don't mean that at all," I says.

"Well you just said you wanted to write the dang dialogue like a song, with rhymes."

"I said just the opposite—write the dang *songs* as dialogue. *Without* rhymes. People don't talk in rhyme. I want to have an underlying unsuspected rhythm underneath the dialogue when I'm ready for a song, like a cable running along underneath Powell Street—then I can hook on to it any time I wish without the audience realizing it."

"Without rhymes, huh. 'In the wigwam of Nakomis, by the big sea shining water, lived a something Indian maiden, something, something gitchy goomie'? Like that, you mean?"

"No, Ernie. I only think there's a way of making rhythmic dialogue get you unsuspectingly into song, in fact serve as either dialogue or song. The rhythm could make it perfectly acceptable song whenever you want to reveal that rhythm, and the fact that there's no rhyme makes it perfectly acceptable dialogue in the meantime."

"What happens at the ends of the lines? When I hear a line about 'the fair young daughter of Nakomis' I want to hear something about 'sitting there upon her tokus,' not 'by the shining gitchy goomie.'"

"There won't be any 'ends of the lines'—they'll disappear if I can figure out the proper rhythm tricks—sleight of hand, you could say. By the way, 'Nakomis' doesn't rhyme with 'tokus.'"

"Okay."

"And you got to introduce the rhythm naturally."

"You mean the garbage man drops the can in rhythm and somebody starts to sing in that tempo?" Ernie says. "Seems to me I seen that some place."

"I don't mean that at all," I says. "I mean a girl jabbing at an embroidery hoop, or a train, maybe."

"Why would a girl be jabbing at a train?"

"I just mean a train. A train coming by."

"Okay," says Ernie. "But you got a job on your hands. And I don't believe in having to justify songs. People come to a musical knowing the actors are going to sing instead of talk and the orchestra is sitting there in the pit for that purpose."

"Okay," I says, "I'll only 'justify the music' when it's natural to do so. And I never said I didn't have a job on my hands."

And so it went. Only once did either of us raise his voice in anger and then it wasn't Ernie. We had just exhausted

45 ]

any possibility of finding a finished script in my latest version—draft number umptiump. I was really discouraged and Ernie didn't make me feel any better by jumping on a reference I made to "the show." "What show?" he says. "We aren't even close to having a show. We don't know the people yet nor where they go nor what they do. And it ain't funny yet." So I blew, and as is usual in such a case, I identified with two parts, one part hero and one part "pore soul."

"Okay Ernie," yells the "pore soul," "you'll see. I may not have a show yet but I got a beginning and an end. And a show is going to be put between that beginning and that end and it'll be the love story of Harold Hill, phony band leader, and Marian, the Librarian!"

"When you find out who she is, lemme know."

"I will!" The "hero" took over: "And when I finish this show," I hollers, Ernie following my hand with some confusion on his face, not knowing that the picture of Alvin Tank and us band boys I was pointing at was the center-field bleachers and that I was now Babe Ruth that glorious day in Chicago, "it'll be a home run, for your information! It won't be a hit, Ernie, it'll be a *smash* hit and you remember what I'm saying!"

Ernie was calm. "That's the difference between us," he says. "You're a dedicated man. I just want to make a buck."

One day late in the summer after we had finished still another new version and hadn't liked it, Ernie sucked in a supply of wind to start spraying out some words. Nothing happened. For the first and only time in my memory, Ernie

Martin said, "Ah—." And stopped. It was terrifying. Like you'd be going along in a DC-7 at 20,000 feet and all four motors quit simultaneously without a warning sputter of any kind. Like the classic joke about the lighthouse keeper whose big alarm rang out every hour on the hour, till one time at three in the morning it didn't ring, and the guy sprang out of bed yelling, *"What was that?"* In about five minutes Ernie went home.

He never told me he was giving up. He didn't have to tell me.

We met a few times more and went through the motions. Then he had to go back to New York, he says.

Next day I stuck a blank piece of paper in the machine but I couldn't get started no matter what I did. I couldn't even write about Iowa. But I couldn't stay away from the dang typewriter, either—I was committed. Friend, I says, ya got trouble.

# *Chapter Three*

It was the stubborn desire to experiment with rhythmic, rhymeless, speak-song that finally got me to select a typewriter key one weary day and punch it. The result three weeks later was a brand-new first scene involving a bunch of salesmen on a train, *speaking* an opening number instead of singing it. Their words were pure *dialogue*, with *no melody* and *no rhyme*. The effect was song, though, because of the underlying rhythm—the rhythm of the train. While I was at it, besides establishing the 1912 period and something about its characteristics, I sneaked into this opening speak-song considerable exposition—often a painful part of a play because of the latecomers stepping all over you while you're trying to find out what's going on.

When I leaned back to take a look I felt pretty good about this new opening—almost as though a turning point had been arrived at. I tried phoning Ernie in New York. He was out of town. I tried Cy. I found him just checking into a New York hospital for some slight hemstitching he had been putting off. I read him the train scene over the phone and he was as enthusiastic as a guy can be with an ether cone over his nose. September came. And October came. And Rini and I were doing a platform evening in a small town in Kansas called Great Bend. Three o'clock in the morning the phone rang and on it were a very excited Cy and Ernie, word-spraying me just like old times.

E: "Just sold *Music Man* to CBS!"

C: "For a one-shot."

"On a TV super two-hour spec-by-God-tac-u-lar!"

"For 100,000 G's!"

"Went right to Paley and Stanton at CBS."

"And the head guys of both the agency and the client!"

"All we need is you to say yes."

"This last draft you sent is pretty good!"

"Cy loves that train thing I haven't heard yet."

"We think we can make TV history."

"They're talking about pre-empting the Sullivan time!"

"Making a two-hour show!"

"The first presentation of an original Broadway musical comedy in TV history."

"Newsy, huh?" ("Great! Let's do it!")

"Hope you're agreeable." ("I am, I am!" I says. "It's great! Let's do it!")

"Because even if you're not happy about it we got to do it anyway."

"We already said yes." ("Wonderful!")

"So we'll have to go ahead."

"But we hope you're happy." ("I'm happy! I'm thrilled!")

"Think it over."

"You'll be thrilled about it when you think it over." ("I don't have to think it—")

"Naturally you'd rather do it on Broadway."

"So would we."

"But this ain't bad." ("I should say not. I love—")

"Think it over."

"Get used to the idea, Mere."

"You'll be happy with it, Mere."

"Love to Rini."

A week later back in Los Angeles I was at the NBC Studios still doing the Beethoven bit for the listeners dear when I got called to the phone. It was "long distance"! So naturally I dropped the world's greatest symphony— Beethoven's Ninth—like it was an elevator button on a cold day. It was Cy and Ernie.

"Deal's off," Cy says. "Couldn't agree on the casting with the agency. We told the agency 'Who needs your okay on casting? Either we're the producers or we aren't.'"

"They called back this morning okaying everything," Ernie says, "but we said 'Too late.' Three weeks later they'd be trying to run something else, so we pulled out. Sorry, Mere. Be talkin' to you."

November. December. *The Music Man* now entered his fifth year of incubation. I was really getting Iowa-stubborn about the talking-rhymeless-rhythm songs as being the way I was determined to bridge dialogue and song. If it works with The Train, why not try it with some other songs? Like maybe a piano lesson?

It was some time later in January when somebody sent me a small clipping from *The New York Times: Feuer and Martin have tabled* The Music Man *in order to concentrate on other plans.*

February was usually a good month for me. I spent it badly the year of '56, however, trying to get a draft together that would accommodate the new stuff I liked and still pare down some of the awful overlength. At the end of the month I had a new draft and it wasn't any two hours too long either—it was two hours-and-a-half too long. The stickler was still the spastic boy. When you have a twelve-year-old character with a brilliant mind locked up in a body with no muscular control to where everyone takes for granted he's crazy, as people did in 1912 (and still do, far too many of them), you have an awful time keeping such a boy from not only stealing his scenes, as Cy warned, but from stealing the whole show. I even tried one draft where the audience never saw him on stage at all. The love story, meanwhile, was getting stronger, a lot stronger, but you'd never notice it with that wheel-chair kid in the show. I wasn't quitting on him, but I was kind of miserable. Then one day Jesse Lasky asked me to come over to his office on the M-G-M lot.

I had never met Mr. Lasky before. He was about as fine a man as I ever met and gentle and kind besides. He held a copy of my book *And There I Stood with My*

*Piccolo* in his hand as we talked. There was a lot of stuff in there about my experiences with Sousa's band. It seemed that Jesse had an idea going that he couldn't get backing for. He wanted to make a picture called *The Big Brass Band* that would tell about the tremendous band activities in American schools today. His hero would, in the course of the story, form an All-American Band selected through local contests, consisting of the two best instrumentalists in every state, the result being a crack hundred-piece outfit. In fact Jesse was actually going to form such a band—had the machinery all ready in all the states, through a very enthusiastic organization he had already formed out of bandmasters and music educators throughout the country. What he wanted from me was a march for the climactic finale.

He was quite cheered up by my reaction to the idea and I was cheered up by his interest in me—two discouraged guys whose difficulties formed a mutual bond, as you could say. A day or two later Jesse came over to our house and Rini and I performed the latest version of *The Music Man* for him. He was a happy audience and enthusiastic about the picture possibilities. Suddenly he stuck out his hand. "Let's pair up," he says, "stick the projects together and see what happens." We shook hands on it—immediately began talking excitedly about how *The Music Man* might have a son or a grandson to bring us down to the present day and maybe hook on to Jesse's All-American Band idea. Within a week, however, Jesse reversed him-self—said we were going too far under the house for our eggs. "The periods and the ideas have nothing in common and we'll end up ruining *The Music Man,* which already strikes me as being too long as it is."

I nodded.

"My idea," says Jesse, "would be to do *two* pictures— produce a double feature. I don't think a 'program' production like that has ever been done. *The Music Man* would start the bill and *The Big Brass Band* as a straight documentary would finish it!"

Well that sounded just great to me and seeing as how we both take from the same agent, we called up our representative and asked him over to our house the following night to hear the latest draft of *The Music Man* as the opening gun in our plan. Our representative not only came but he brought fourteen other men with him from his office. Rini and I performed a somewhat cut version which, even so, seemed to take three days. During that whole time there wasn't a sound in the room—not a laugh, not a chuckle, not even a snick. And no reaction at all to the songs. Jesse tried a few prop reactions in the beginning, then just sat there in the corner pale as a ghost, completely gagged by the fantastic silence that froze every vibration in the room except my voice droning on and on. I wanted to quit a dozen times but didn't know how. Rini got so mad she could hardly see straight and sang like an angel.

After the others had gone, Jesse did his best to cheer us up by recalling what a miserable time he'd had with *The Great Caruso,* which was turned down by everybody and his brother before M-G-M finally did Jesse a favor and let him make it into one of their greatest successes.

It got to be June after a while. I had written *The Music Man* twice more, from the gym opening, now preceded by The Train, to the band finale I had so much faith in, still troubling with the spastic boy, still experimenting with trying to translate plain dialogue into speak-songs. I was also still trying to attract "listeners dear" for my friend Mr. Beethoven on NBC radio, which, plus my ASCAP income and the royalty from "May the Good Lord Bless and Keep You," was blessing us and keeping us to the extent that I could leave the rest of the time for plowing with my Iowa musical comedy. Jesse was busy and making progress, having completed a very good documentary film of his *Big Brass Band* with Jimmy Stewart narrating, but without getting the All-American Band actually formed and into the picture—which was the thing he had his heart set on. He always came up smiling, though, and it was a swell smile—that Lasky one. The more stumbling blocks he ran into the harder he worked, refusing to accept any compromise. As time went on we exchanged letters dissolving our brief "handshake" partnership. On the bottom of my letter Jesse scribbled under his name *And good luck! And God bless you!*

Well if Jesse can keep on, I can keep on, I says to myself, as long as I got an opening and a closing.

# Chapter Four

We had viewed that year, so far, as passengers in a giant rolly-coaster traveling in Fantasia—now in the gold and white towers high in the clouds, now in the dripping underground bat-cave, sets and lighting by Hogarth. And we hadn't reached autumn yet. How could one and the same project beget such high hope and such blank despair in such small segments of elapsed time? During that summer, for instance, Cy Feuer came out to California and stopped over to the house for a sort of informal official good-by and look what happened all within four days. We were tying it off in the driveway: Cy told me a funny joke to deflate the tension; Cy said how sorry he was things didn't work out; that we were separating with no obligation on either side—I was welcome to *The Music Man* title for what it was worth; Cy ruefully mentioned how easy it had been for him to sell it for TV that time because he had such faith in it; Cy got an idea and dashed into the house to make a phone call; he dashed out again telling me to go immediately to Hillcrest Country Club where he had just steamed up Sol Siegel, who was currently producing *Philadelphia Story* for Metro, with a stable including Sinatra, Crosby, Grace Kelly and Johnny Patrick. ("Could *he* help you lick the book! He wrote *Tea House!*"); Cy drove off; I met Mr. Siegel at Hillcrest; he and his wife came the following night to our house; Rini and I rendered the score for them and ad-libbed the book; Sol and his wife didn't leave till three o'clock in the morning—"starry-eyed" would not be too strong a word to describe the way they looked— UP; I sent Sol the current draft of the script next day; UP—Sol called the day after—said he talked to Crosby and was seeing his top representative that afternoon—UP; next day a letter from Sol: *Crosby interests not interested at this time;* DOWN-ish; *however,* the message continued, *still trying.* UP-ish. Thirty days later, accompanied by a regretful note, my script returned by special messenger; DOWN.

Don Quinn was going to help me lick the book. UP. Don Quinn had to go to Honolulu. DOWN. Ray Bolger came over and loved the score. UP. Ray Bolger signed for a solid year of TV, not available. DOWN. Get a great idea which involves changing Marian from a Librarian to a school teacher. UP. Rewrite everything to fit the new idea and it doesn't work. DOWN. Nuts.

August. Still 1956. Rini and I were so numb reading the different versions of this *Music Man* to each other we were paralyzed on the subject. August was the month I had agreed to write and conduct the music for *The California*

[ 56

*Story* downt San Diego, a huge-size dramatic and musical pageant with thirteen hundred actors and two thousand horses. (Rini says every time I tell it I add a couple hundred horses. Anyway, they had twenty mules in one team, I *know* that.) So we turned loose of *The Music Man* and for the first time in four and a half years we're shed of Harold Hill. We resolved not to look at the gol-darn script for the whole two weeks we're in San Diego.

Well. Down there the first person we met was a six-foot-four skinny, extrovert of a homemade apple-pie smile on stilts, like we'd known him all our lives, by the name of Franklin Lacey, who was adapting and otherwise trouble-shooting the book of this *California Story* pageant. And he is a hollerer! It was a frantic couple weeks down there but extremely successful and therefore a big morale booster for Rini and me.

Twenty-four hours after the pageant's final performance and cast party, Rini and I were sitting on top of the San Jacinto mountains on that same porch up in Idyllwild, pointing out to Franklin the approximate place in between the peaks where Feuer and Martin had passed on their intrepid flight to the Oak Leaf Café a year and a half before. And beside me is a stack of manuscript approximately two feet high representing the current working drafts of *The Music Man*. I had regained some objectivity by my completely contrasting activity the past two weeks in San Diego and I managed to partly narrate and partly read the story to Franklin with some considerable enthusiasm, sitting there on the porch. The beginning and the end remained; "Professor" Harold Hill was still The Boy; Marian, the Librarian, was still The Girl. The janitor's spastic son was still the subplot. Mayor Shinn was a kind of heavy, his wife Eulalie was the scatter-brain social leader of River City; Charley Cowell, an anvil salesman, was emerging as Harold's envious rival, Tommy, the "Kilroy" juvenile, and Zaneeta, the Mayor's apple-of-his-eye daughter, were still the sub-love story; and the crochety school board still became an inseparable barbershop quartette as Harold Hill's first "miracle" in River City. As I look back now, with the simple elements I had from practically the very first draft, it seems almost impossible that I could have spent so long a time cluttering up this simple story instead of clearing it up. But then you don't know how glued I was to the spastic-boy subplot—how badly I wanted to tell on a stage that spastics are muscularly retarded not mentally.

Well, Franklin listened and laughed heartily and cried a little in the right places and otherwise reacted loudly and happily as we sat there that bright morning hollering at each other in the pines. Now Franklin, as it turned out, was not only a former stage manager, a play-doctor, a playwright, and a former child-prodigy lecturer, but also was a part-time professor in a rather famous private California school wherein there were a couple *spastic children.* This was partly fortunate, because it made Franklin immediately enthusiatic about *The Music Man,* and partly unfortunate because he gave me such strong support with respect to my spastic subplot, which was really the rock in the peanut brittle only I didn't know it yet. Anyway, Franklin was the brightest thing that had happened in our lives for a long time. With great optimism and confidence he says, "I can wade you through this jungle overnight. I can see how the scenes should follow as clearly as if I was seeing this show on the stage!"

The rest of the day we sat there on the porch and happily played the game of now-you-tell-me-the-story-of-the-Music-Man-in-the-fewest-possible-words, that same old game Rini and I had not only played so much with Cy and with Ernie, but also with my brother Cedric and with his wife Lois, and with my neighbor Frank and his wife Margaret, and with our other neighbor Fred Zinnemann and his wife Renée—and also with the Allens, the Vincents, the Seatons, the Gangs, the Tyres, the Freedmans, the Dailards, the Goodwins, the Scudders, the Perrieres, the Hogues, the Moffitts, the Fines, Abe Meyer, Freeman Ambrose, the Mamoulians, the Quinns, Sterling Holloway, George Gruskin, our dachshund Piccolo, our alley cat Cookie, and our Bavarian housekeeper Josephine who, by the way, never bothered to learn English, overlooking the fact that at the same time she was forgetting her German. (Sample Josephinese: "Clowdia Goldberg," meaning Claudette Colbert; "I'll follow my Ziegfreid heart"; "I am disgusting mit you," meaning I will discuss it with you. Nothing wrong with her imagination though—one day she says to Rini, "Don't buy dot cat-food in dot can. Today Cookie sniffs—walks away. 'Eat it yourself,' she says to me.")

Franklin exaggerated when he said he could give me an outline of the scenes in one day—it took him two. And his knowledge of stagecraft was tremendously helpful. I always kept an outline on a blackboard I had in the music

room at home, upon which I'd learned from Ernie Martin
to draw the scenes: in One (down near the "footlights")
like this ⊂▭⊃ and the deeper scenes, like in Two or
Three or even Full, like this ▭ . Then you could
lay on the musical numbers in any given scene like this
▯▮▮▮ and that way you could keep the whole show
and the contrasts clear in your mind at a glance—also the
relative length of the first and second acts and the ratios
of talk and music—production numbers—ballet—and so on.
(I still have the final blackboard version of the show we
chalked up there before Rini and I went to New York for
the last hitch—can't quite bring myself to erase it.) Franklin would point out stagecraft methods where you could,
if necessary, follow one full-stage scene with another:
▭ ▭ without necessarily having to always
arrange a smaller scene in between: ▭—▭ in
order to allow the stage crew time to change the scenery.

Well, we worked out a system, actually it worked itself
out, whereby I would write all day, and Franklin would
come over around four, five o'clock and I'd scream and
holler the scenes I had put down on the paper since yesterday. And he'd scream and holler enthusiastic agreement
or enthusiastic disagreement. Then one way or the other,
I'd worry about it during the night, sleep some, and make
changes and go ahead till four, five o'clock the next afternoon. The signal to stop was when Franklin banged on the
door. Then the hollering would begin again. In this manner
I got a completely new draft written down on the paper,
final-typed and in carbon, too, because my secretary Joan

[ 60

Pollak was and always has been hopelessly stage-struck and didn't have any more normal brains therefore than to sit there and keep typing the stuff as long as I was hunting-and-pecking in the next room even though she could have gotten the same salary I was now paying her by merely standing in the Unemployment Relief line a few minutes a week.

So went September. One day, in my constant preoccupation with cudgeling the brain for authentic recall, I got down a lot of stuff about the evils of the pool hall and some similar social scourges of 1912. This grew into a diatribe of some length and in reading it over I realized I had at last actually applied my lyric writer's ear to a hunk of dialogue without consciously intending to do so. Well. In fact the whole pool-hall speech would pass the standards of a good honest lyric, I thought, it having a fine rhythmic feel to it. Its words fell trippingly off the tongue without consonant bumping into consonant and without any embarrassing nonsustainable syllables showing up at the ends. And it didn't rhyme! So I started to work out an accompaniment—*not a tune, an accompaniment.* And I want to tell you that I've had days go by fast, but that day when Franklin hammered on the music-room door and I hollered "tomorrow," I'll swear it seemed like he just stepped back from that door and hammered again—that's how fast tomorrow came even though I did go to bed. Oh I sleep good but I always wake wide up at three-thirty, four A.M. when I'm working like that. Things seem sharper and clearer to me then than at some other hour—I don't

61 ]

even have to write it down, I remember it—that is if it's any good—and first thing you know it's light and I'm back in the music room with Rini feeding me my vitamin pills and wheat germ and calcium and cod-liver oil—honest— and apple-cider vinegar—two teaspoonful—and papaya and Sanka and stone-ground rye toast to wash all that stuff down with. And there was Franklin banging on the door. I jumped onto the piano and ad-libbed the rhythm accompaniment, *no melody,* and hollered, "Well, you got trouble" at my good friend Franklin, "right here, I say, trouble right here in River City" and I didn't stop for the whole six-page harangue. Rini, who'd been hearing it for two days, stood there beaming; Piccolo was barking her brains out. Even our cat Cookie deigned to turn her head passing by the door. Joan grabbed the paper as I finished and began typing the lyrics like mad and Josephine fell up against the jamb and says, "Vare yoo could vind such a aktor to zing zuch a long scrabbling?" And did she have something there!

Anyway, it was another turning point to have faith in—you can sure recognize them, at least you can when you're as hungry for them as I was—and I started in at Act One, Scene Three, saying to myself, *This time sure, if I can ever get to going.* My priming essay was nice and short this time—a description of

### THE BRAKEMAN'S HAND

Whenever I stir up my memory I continue to be impressed by the splendid manner in which, therein, one slight, nonchalant man in gold watch chain and overalls, mittened and in visored hood, appears to dangle, as through some wireless control, a mile-long freight train at the end of one gracefully circling hand—a Mayo fiddling with his scalpel, a Heifetz toying with his bow, a Manolete noodling with his rapier, contemptuously and effortlessly reducing yonder advancing earthquake-on-wheels to a whispering, hat-in-hand simper of a bridegroom approaching tiptoe, creaking apologetic course, swaying ever so slightly, off-balance a bit (more like the father of the bride than the groom with perhaps one too many? Trying to cope with the pace of a too-slow wedding march?) but moving on, nevertheless, straight to the shy little frightened Lillian Gish caboose waiting all of a dark red blush, yet standing her ground with that particular kind of female courage a gentlewoman used to have to have in my generation. And had. Without giving away an ounce of her modesty or graces either. No. I don't look down on today's kids at all. *But I'll never forgive the little monsters not only for not being thrilled to the marrow of their arrogant, mealy little bones at such a magnificent sight but for yawning in my face when I'm pointing it out to them.*

# Chapter Five

During the course of getting the resulting draft down on the paper I not only incorporated "Ya Got Trouble" into the first act, but, using that same rhythm and meter, I also wrote a similar-type spoken intro to "Seventy-Six Trombones" and a complete parody version of "Trouble" for the jealous salesman to fling back in Harold's teeth by way of a second-act reprise. This only got into the show once—in Philadelphia when Paul Reed proved himself a hero and a trouper by getting up in it in a few hours and delivering it flawlessly at the performance that night—but it served its purpose during that writing period, drawing the book and lyrics closer together as one piece, and also it was a good exercise making my particular kind of rhythmic dialogue interchangeable with song. In that draft I also wrote a new song for Harold with a speak-song intro called "The Sadder But Wiser Girl." Actually I wrote this in counterpoint to Marian's song about her long-dreamed-of "White Knight." In fact, in that particular draft the simultaneous singing of those two songs at either end of the footbridge was the first-act finale. Actually, there is so much counterpoint (one melody against another) in the score that Bob Fosse, the famous choreographer, turned down *The Music Man* on the grounds that the score all sounded alike to him. Eventually, however, the counterpoint rendition of White Knight and Sadder But Wiser got cut out completely. With the exception of when Rini and I occasionally get on at parties, no use was ever made of the fact that these songs fit together.

It is now October. Still '56. And presently it got to be November. Franklin and I were still hollering at each other at four o'clock every afternoon and Joan was still clobbering away at the typewriter and Rini and I were still periodically using our good, kind friends' ears when ours gave out. And beginning with November, I started to put down on the paper Draft #32 of *The Music Man*. Again, Act One, Scene One, for criminy sakes, with the exception of The Train and my other speak-song scenes. But my bones vibrated with a kind of happy buzzing this time. Shortly before Thanksgiving I had a brand-new first act down on paper that felt mostly in one piece.

And then one morning Josephine did what she never did before—she charged into the music room with the door shut and me sitting in there hunting-and-pecking. Her face was white and she could only point back of her toward the front door. "Duh Mister Martin" she finally says in a daze. Now I know a Bill Martin on the Board of Directors of the Big Brothers philanthropic group I belong to. That was the only Mr. Martin I could think of in our part of the world,

65 ]

but there was nothing about that Martin to cause Josephine
to turn up in this amazing condition. I followed her out
the door to the stairs leading up to the front hall. Rini,
having been struck by the thought of an entirely different
Mr. Martin, followed right behind me, completely oblivi-
ous to the cold cream she had on her face and the fact
that she had her hair up in those things and was standing
there in her underskirt. It was Ernie all right. We looked
up at him standing there at the head of the stairs like he
was The Boy from Out There, only instead of his saying
"Take me to your leader" he says, "Hi Rini. Hi Mere. You
got anything to drink? Any strawberry pop or anything?
I tried to get you for a while on your phone," he says, "but
the line was busy and I thought this was pretty important
so I thought I'd drive on over and tell you about it. Ever
hear of a book called *Indian Joe?* Book-of-the-Month Club
couple years back. Well Cy and I got the rights, see. Has
to do with contemporary Indian life—American Indians up
in Montana—hogans and firewater and all that stuff, and
we're out at M-G-M now about to produce this *Indian
Joe* into a picture, but in the meantime we got M-G-M's
blessing to do it first as a Broadway musical and the best
screenwriter in the business is Krasna who everybody has
always tried to get him to do a Broadway show and he
always said no dice—sarsaparilla'd be fine if you haven't
got any strawberry pop, or even Coke—that was because
he never ran into a property that appealed to him, I suppose, but anyway he's home right now writing pages and
he'd like to see you right away—today if possible. See, Cy
and I went down the whole list of words-and-music guys—

it's not Cole's dish, though we feel strongly about Irving
Berlin, who may want very much to do this, but after
noodling around for some time—this was no impulsive decision—we decided you were our number one choice to do
words and music. We got the theatre a'ready—go into rehearsals August fifteenth of 1957—and there's your chance
to learn about Broadway from the top in a guaranteed hit
with everything solid gold all the way, the best writer,
Book-a'-the-Month story that's *news*, the best company,
theatre, backing, everything top drawer, top notch, top
grade. Here's Krasna's phone number, he's dying to talk
to you."

After a false start in falsetto, I says, "Pretty flattering the
way you bounced me up at the head of the list there.
Those other names you threw at me were not chopped
liver, you know."

"Cy keeps saying you're the best words-and-music man
in the business and I guess it isn't any secret because he
tells it to everybody he runs into. Maybe a little ginger
ale? If you haven't got any Coca-Cola."

I hurried up the steps. Ernie followed me into the den
where I gave him a glass of tonic. Rini had said hello and
disappeared in a hurry when she realized her principal
apparel was face cream and curlers. "Well you thank Cy
for me," I says. "And you tell him I've got some new rhymeless wonders like The Train I'm anxious for him to hear.
Which reminds me. I don't see how I can do this Indian
project with you guys. I got a project, remember?"

"You mean *The Music Man?*" Ernie says. "I thought
you gave that up."

"*I* didn't," I says, "*you* did."

"You mean you licked the book?" says Ernie.

"Comeer," I says, grabbing him by the coat and pulling him downstairs into the music room and pushing him into his familiar chair that had not felt his sphaghetti-upholstered *derrière* for exactly one year four months and two days. I then turned on my own word-sprayer and beginning with Act One, Scene One, Draft #32, I started with The Train he hadn't heard yet. "You can talk, you can talk, you can bicker, you can talk, you can talk, talk, talk, talk, bicker, bicker, bicker, you can talk all you wanna but it's different than it was!" And I didn't stop till the curtain dropped on Harold Hill on one side of the footbridge singing "The Sadder But Wiser Girl" with Marian at the other side of the bridge (Rini had a dress on by now) singing "My White Knight," which was the First Act finale at the time.

"Mere," Ernie says, "I'm proud a' ya. And you know that gitchy-goomie Nakomis stuff is the greatest?"

"Thanks, Ernie," I says. "And I thank your ghost who has been occasionally butting in around here in your absence, quoting Egri to me and some other very solid principles of your own about level and such as that."

"I still say you should do our show," says Ernie. "Without hearing the second act I can tell you right now Cy and I will produce this *Music Man* for you in 1958, but meanwhile we're all tied up to do this Indian show first and Krasna's already writing pages waiting to talk to you."

"I know."

"But wouldn't you rather have two Broadway hits than

one? Learn about Broadway from the top? A major musical comedy, with Krasna and Jo Mielziner and all the top people in the business? At least come over to my office and let me outline the show for you so you'll know what you're turning down."

I spent practically the whole next day in Ernie's office at M-G-M while he paced up and down and sprayed me with a fine-sounding musical comedy book—all ad-lib of course, but convincing. Convincing? Irresistible. Almost. (If the subsequent Broadway version had been as convincing as Ernie's that day, it would have been a smash hit.)

"I got too much steam up on *Music Man*, Ernie," I says, "can't just walk away from it like that. Can't turn it on and off that fast. Can't get intense enough about some other completely different kind of a show just now. And if I can't get intense about it, how can the stuff I write be any good?"

"Look Mere, don't answer me now. Talk it over with Rini. Take your time. Two weeks? Three weeks?"

I figured I could finish the new second act of *Music Man* in three weeks. "Okay, Ernie," I says. "Call you on Monday, three weeks from today."

"Great, Mere," he says. "Three weeks from Monday around eleven thirty, twelve o'clock."

My best friends said grab it—Feuer and Martin never had a flop. Norman Krasna's the best in the business. Don't be a chump. Do the Indian thing now—look at the Broadway experience you'll get, with the absolutely top guys. You so rich you can turn down a guaranteed Broadway Feuer and Martin musical comedy smash hit? So you only get four per cent for music and lyrics being as it's your first time out. Don't forget that comes *off the top*. They'll surely play $70,000 grossers like the Shubert or the Hellinger. That's twenty-eight hundred bucks a week! *Six thousand a week* when the road company starts. And what about records? The cast album could go half a million gross by itself. That's maybe a hundred and fifty thousand bucks more. And sheet music. And singles. And other albums. And ASCAP. And *the picture*. Grab it man, grab it.

Rini says, "Darling, I sure don't want to stir you wrong, but I say the heck with it. You finish *The Music Man*."

Well being as I had three weeks before I had to decide, I put the whole thing out of my mind and finished the second act.

It would really be square to give you the old Frank Merriwell finish here, and try to tell you that on that exact Monday morning at eleven forty-five, three weeks later to the day, I wrote *Curtain* on the new second act. Besides, I made up my mind when I started writing this account it wouldn't be worth reading unless I put down everything just like it happened.

So I have to tell that three weeks later to the day on Monday morning at eleven forty-five I wrote *Curtain*, looked at my watch and hollered, "Rini, I'm done."

After we congratulated each other I says, "Rini. You know Frank Loesser's big hit musical *Most Happy Fella?* It's produced by a guy named Kermit Bloomgarden. Wonder if he'd be interested in producing *The Music Man?*"

"You don't have to call Ernie for ten more minutes," Rini says. "Call up Mr. Bloomgarden and ask him."

"I will," I says.

His office located him in a theatre some place. I could hear rehearsing going on. "Of course they'd find him," Rini says, "it's 'long distance'!"

"Hello Mr. Bloomgarden!" I says, hollering even louder than I do in a room, another thing long distance always seems to do to people. Now Cy and Ernie have a rapid-fire delivery, but we Hawkeyes yield to no one when it comes to being long-winded. I unreeled the whole story to Mr. Bloomgarden about Ernie and Cy asking me to do the score for their new show, about Ernie expecting my answer today, about my just finishing the new draft, about my friends' opinions, about my agent's opinion, and after quite a while when I stopped for a breath Mr. Bloomgarden said, "Pardon me, have we ever met?" (My only consolation here was that he never heard of Art Linkletter either.)

I say, "No sir, I don't believe so."

He says, "All this sounds very interesting. Can't you send me the book?"

I says no I couldn't because there was a lot of stuff in there like seven salesmen imitating the sound of a 1912 train which took the place of what would normally be the opening number—only there wasn't any tune here and no singing, not even any rhymes, and this number not only imitated the sound of a train but it also got rid of the exposition which is always—or at least pretty generally—boring in a show and hard to rise above—and there were other musical numbers like that, where it wouldn't mean

71 ]

much just reading them off the paper, whereas Rini and I had worked out a way to demonstrate these songs—in fact we did the whole show, took all the parts and sang all the songs. When I stopped for a moment to see if we were still connected he said, "Fine. I'll give you all the time you want any night this week."

I say, "How about Wednesday?"

And he says, "Fine—Wednesday night at Herb Greene's apartment at 200 West 58th Street. Twelve midnight. That will give Herb a chance to get home from conducting *Most Happy Fella*."

I thanked him, hung up and called Ernie.

"Well I'll be doggoned," Ernie says.

I says, "Yeah."

Ernie says, "Well don't say no yet. Bloomgarden may not like your show. He may not like you. You may not like him. Lots of things can happen. Cy is in our New York office. Go see him Thursday morning after you do the audition."

"Okay," I says, "but it won't be too early. We're not starting the audition till midnight and the script runs a little long."

"You don't say."

# Chapter Six

Well, Rini and I had a hard time sitting around in the Waldorf waiting for midnight to arrive. We got to the Greenes' apartment a little early. A very nice lady at the door turned out to be Mrs. Greene and we went in. The living room had an electric organ in one corner—which Cole Porter had given Mr. Greene after *Silk Stockings,* we found out later—and a beautiful Steinway grand against the outside wall by the window. The rest of the room was occupied by a long couch and coffee table, a couple chairs, a desk, and some very elaborate recording and playback equipment. I noticed out in the hall when we came in where Herb Greene had hung up posters from the hit shows he had been connected with: *Guys and Dolls, Can Can, Silk Stockings, Most Happy Fella* and quite a few more. I wondered if *The Music Man* would ever be up on that wall. He'd also be the guy who'd have to throw that downbeat on our opening night, too. I shuddered and changed the subject to myself.

In a couple moments he came in. Friendliness in his large smile, youth in his physical movement—thirty-four, thirty-five?—five feet ten?—curly dark hair, extrovertism in his white leather coat and black gold-headed cane—a brother pedestrian?—and independence in the large dill pickle he had been eating like an ice-cream cone walking along the street—on such a night? He *was* a pedestrian. The wind whistled around the corner of the building. His apartment was on the top floor. Mr. Greene asked me to try the piano. A pip, it was. Herb's wife, it developed, is a concert pianist.

Well, in a short while the bell rang and in came this not tall well-proportioned nice-looking fellow very well dressed—looked anywhere around the late forties there in the apartment which didn't have too much light in it except over the piano music-rack. That was our first look at Kermit Bloomgarden. He said Hodado and that was about all. It wasn't much of a night for talking—sleety, cold, blowy outside, and painful, nervous, tense and a little unreal inside— at least it was for me. December 19th it was, 1956. My Rini was, of course, tense and unreal feeling too, but I didn't have to worry about her getting nervous—she gets mad. I'm always nervous at the beginning. If all goes well right off, I get over it. If not, I lose my courage and start collecting that cotton in the mouth. Cotton mather, I call it because that's what it feels like—mather. Mr. Allentuck was there, also Anne Gordon, Betty Hart and Vaughan Bellaver. All from the Bloomgarden office. The pleasantries were short. Nobody really wanted to be there anyway on such a night at such an hour but there we were, so let's go. The New

York City steam heat was on full blast so in spite of the sleety night the window was open near the piano which let in the street noise from down on Seventh Avenue. I asked Mr. Greene if he'd close the window because it was hard to concentrate against that noise and also hard for the people to hear. "I have a lyric show," I says, "and I'd like to be sure the words are all heard."

"Be pretty stuffy in here," somebody said. "We're smoking, you know."

I didn't say any more and neither did anybody else. Mr. Greene closed the window. I hit a few chords on the piano to simulate an overture.

"Curtain up," I says, stealing a last look at Mr. Bloomgarden. He favored me with what I have since learned is legendary in the trade: The Bloomgarden Look, which, according to Thornton Wilder for one, would "tunnel through an Alp." I breathed in and started with The Train.

"You can talk, you can talk, you can bicker, you can talk, you can talk, talk, talk, talk, bicker, bicker, bicker, you can talk all you wanna but it's different than it was."

Rini: (at the top of her lungs, simulating the extra volume and higher pitch of a train at a crossing) "No it ain't, no it ain't, but you gotta know the territory!"

The next few lines were drowned out by Herb Greene, but I never lost a piece of a lyric more gladly, because his interruption was a happy hoot of a yelping belt I'm sure you could have heard in Carnegie Hall a block down the street. I remember thinking: What do you know, no mather!, before slipping happily into the stream of general approval which took on a whole lot of character unbelievably fast. And it got stronger and stronger. The ten-minute break we took between acts didn't slow anything up either. We were in, that's all. Everything paid off—the lyrics—the jokes—the tunes—the love story. And three and a half hours later at half past four in the morning when I hollered "Curtain," Herb and Kermit and Max and Betty and Vaughan and Anne and Rini and I and my soaking sweaty shirt were hugging and hollering and slapping backs and laughing and screaming all at the same time.

And then Kermit and I really got acquainted. Two pounds of sturgeon and a couple dozen bagels later we left just as it was starting to get light.

There was something very familiar for Rini and me in that early-morning cab ride to the Waldorf, with our same idiot smiles back in place and our same grinning head-shaking disbelief. When we finally got to sleep we really corked off out of emotional exhaustion.

It was hard to struggle awake next morning when the phone rang. No wonder, it was only nine o'clock. Kermit's voice was very sharp and clear and wide awake. "Good morning," he says. "Woke up my wife last night when I got home, breaking a rule of a good many years. Had to tell her about last night. She got so excited we ended up in the kitchen with scrambled eggs and I haven't been to bed yet. Can you come over? I'm at the office."

We had never been to Kermit's office before. That seems unbelievable now—can hardly think back that far. We had a time finding it, I recall, because the street number is 1545 Broadway which is a movie theatre. We finally found a small pair of doors back of the box office—you almost have to buy a ticket to get in—and went up to the second floor. Kermit's office is located behind that great block-long sign which hides the second floor of all the buildings on the west side of Broadway between 45th Street and 46th Street, the signboard that was first erected for the huge super-spectacular sign of *Baby Doll* lying there in her block-long crib.

"If we're not on Broadway now, this is about as close as we'll ever get," I whispers to Rini. Kermit said good morning, pointed out the couch for Rini, a chair for me. Max Allentuck came in, and Betty, and Anne, and Lil, and Vaughan, and Shirley. Kermit cleared his throat and said it.

"Meredith," he says, "may I have the privilege of producing your beautiful play?"

Well we had an errand to do, Rini and I, overt the Feuer and Martin office on East 52nd Street, to give the final decision to Cy, as promised. First, though, we wallowed in the wonderful game of "casting" with Herb, Max, Vaughan, Betty and Kermit. "Of course, I see Danny Kaye in the part—"

"He'd be sumpin', wouldn't he? Plus two-million advance at the box office!"

"You know, of course, *who is really* Harold Hill—Dan Dailey. Imagine, where Harold comes out from behind the phony front in the last act. Is that Dan Dailey or not? Hm? *Hm?*"

"You think Gene Kelly would be anything but great in the part?"

77 ]

"Don't ever forget Mr. Broadway, Mr. Two-Million Advance any old day in the week, Mr. Ray Bolger."

And then the offbeat casting—that's the real fun.

"Gimme forty pounds offa Jackie Gleason and *there's* a Harold *Hill*."

"Now just a minute—just a minute—you know who could make you believe the real Hill? Milton Berle, that's who. Ever see Uncle Milty play legit? Only the best actor you ever saw!"

"Uh-uh. No sir. The best actor you ever saw is a guy named Jason Robards and he *sings* a little, did you know that?"

"So does Art Carney. You think he'd be bad? Why he'd tear your heart out."

"Well, you guys can laugh but the guy with the convincing kisser is a little old TV guy by the name of Bert Parks, and if you think I can't get excited about *him* in the role you're crazy."

But Rini and I had our errand to do. It was nearly a mile cross-town but we had to walk—too excited to sit still in a cab. First time we ever walked that Rini's feet didn't hurt—how could anything hurt?

Cy was waiting for us. There wasn't any room for preliminaries. "Kermit's going to do it, Cy," I says.

"He said so?"

"He sure did."

"If he said he'll do it, he'll do it," fell out of Cy's mouth, as great a tribute as any Broadway producer will ever receive from a hot and heavy rival. There's a lot of sparkle razzle-dazzle to show business besides what's up there on the stage. A producer has to play both ends against the middle very often—tell you he's got Sinatra in order to get you, then tell Sinatra he's got *you* in order to get *him*. And tell a writer you're going to produce his play in order to get the revisions started, with the private reservation that you'll produce it providing you like the revisions. But not Bloomgarden. Cy's impulsive kudo said plainly that a lot of producers might tell you they'll do your show, but don't hold your breath till opening night. Not Bloomgarden though. If he says he'll produce it you can now tell your friends.

I was sorry to be so high when Cy was so low but I still had a lot of steam from some place I had to let off. So I jumped over to his piano. "Here's some of the new stuff," I says, and slammed into "Ya Got Trouble" in the loudest holler of my life which is pretty loud. I jumped off the stool at the end and hit the last note on his desk with my hand so hard that it lifted his desk-set three inches in the air and made my little finger sore for a week though I didn't feel it for two days. Anyway I thanked Cy for all those compliments Ernie had told me about. Whereupon Cy told them all over again to my face and we parted on a real sentimental note. At the door he said, "You'll get a top production from Bloomgarden. I think he'll do your show better than we could." If there was anything backhanded in that remark it completely escaped me. Anyway I'm telling you exactly what he said. The three of us embraced and that was it.

The next time I saw Cy—no, I better tell this in order. During lunch that day we took on another new kissin' cousin, Kermit's wife Ginny—Virginia Kaye, professionally. You know her not only from Broadway but from the better TV dramas. She's one of those rare blondes who not only gives you the whips and jingles, but also conveys conviction in her acting—sincerity in her personal impression.

"It's a whole new Kermit," Ginny says. "And you must know by now that he doesn't enthuse too easily. If he were to catch Edwin Booth's Hamlet he might very well go backstage to say to him, 'Very encouraging,' or 'I believe you're on the right track.'"

After lunch we make a plan. "We're all too excited and too near the holidays to do any real work," says Kermit. "I would say our first move is to get a top director. Morton Da Costa or Moss Hart, either one, would certainly be great for the show. Moss lives in my same apartment house. Supposing I set up a date with him sometime the first or second week in January. Can you two go home and get back to New York by then?" We sure could. "You've got a lot of work to do on that book, Meredith. I think you're going to need a collaborator. But we should get the director first so he'll be in on the cutting and rewrite." My ego stumbled a little. Just for a moment.

Postponing any too specific thoughts about the new year waiting up ahead, we left the Bloomgardens as we would close and dear friends—having known Ginny but during the course of one lunch, and Kermit for considerable less than twenty-four hours.

Details of Christmas that next week have faded from my memory to become vague remembrances of overwhelming relief and happiness, too solid to dare to believe in except that it was Christmas, and we, therefore, permitted ourselves to forget the restraint of professional rolly-coaster riders and behave like amateurs.

Two weeks later we were back in New York. Kermit suggested his apartment for the audition this time—larger than Herb's and handy for Moss Hart who lived upstairs; but I urged we stick to Herb's place—for luck—and Herb's it was.

Kermit has a habit we hadn't yet heard about, of inviting, whenever he has any kind of audition coming up, any and all friends he may run into during the day. Crowded onto Herb's couch, organ bench and extra chairs, when we arrived that night, were the Bloomgarden staff, the Fred Coes of TV, the Philip Barry, Jrs., the Martin Jurows, Paul Osborn (the playwright) and his wife, together with eight or ten strangers, dinner party guests of each of these couples. And Kitty and Moss Hart. Being as it was a nine-o'clock affair Herb was absent, conducting *Happy Fella.* I certainly missed his big boffola there at The Train opening but the audience was warm, and gradually got warmer and were extremely gracious about having to set there till one-thirty on account of the show was a little long.

Moss Hart had said he liked the first-act curtain; Kitty had reacted happily, and as near as I could tell, absorbedly; but at the end Mr. Hart had only three things to say. To Rini, "You sang very prettily." To Kermit, "Phone you in the morning." And to me, "Good night."

Next morning Kermit called us to come over. Again nine o'clock and I was sure revising my impression about Broad-

way people lying in bed all morning. Kermit had his thinking cap on as we came in and asked me about a song called
"Chicago" I had taken out of the show. I was so eager to
hear about Moss Hart I didn't give him a very bright
answer before saying, "What did Moss Hart have to say?"
Kermit thought for a moment, his face reacting like a man
who has been jerked from an important subject to an ir-
relevant one.

"Moss?" he says. "Oh. He didn't like it." My stomach got
left behind. Your rolly coaster awaits. Kermit says, "I
thought of a place for that Chicago song in the second act
where it might work great."

"What might?" I says.

" 'Chicago,' " he says.

"What didn't he like about it?" I says. And so help me,
Kermit says, "Who?"

From that time forward Kermit got it almost daily from
big important men in the theatre. "Don't do it, Kermit,"
they told him.

"It's corny, Kermit."

"You'll never lick the book."

But it seemed that there was one old-school guy left in
the entertainment world who used his own judgment.
Can't find many guys around any more in our business who
use their own judgment. Take the music business. Abe
Olman, Saul Bourne, Harry Link, Jack Robbins, Rocco
Vocco—they used to study their market for a few months
and all the available new material; then pick out their
songs on the basis of their own judgments. Then they

stuck with those songs through Hell and high water, plugged the b' jeepers out of them, went up with them or down as the case might be. Same with the Jack Kapps of the record business. But no more. Today a song's got to be a hit record before a publisher will dare publish it. How does he get a record to begin with? Not through anybody's judgment. Usually the price is a thousand to two thousand bucks—under the table. Otherwise a record company will buy a record off of a smaller record company that has already proven itself, rather than anybody using, Heaven forbid, any judgment. No judgment any more; no taste any more; no guts any more. But Kermit Bloomgarden is old-fashioned that way. Like his battered lucky hat.

Kermit wanted Rini to sing the Chicago song for him but Rini wasn't quite ready to change the subject.

"So I sang 'very prettily,' did I?" she says. "Well I say the Lord had His arms around us when Mr. Famous Moss Hart turned us down, Kermit. Do you know what he hung in the closet that night at Herb Greene's? A *mink-lined overcoat*. What would he know about small-town Iowans like us?"

We met that afternoon again. Kermit spoke mainly about my considering getting rid of the spastic boy. Kermit knew the spastic boy had to go, but he also knew the way to lose him was not to give me an ultimatum about it—he knew that just digging that subplot out of there would leave a pretty raw hole. Also he understood my strong feeling about this spastic boy and how important I felt it was to the play. So he never told me for sure we had to lose the kid, preferring to let me find out for myself. However, I suspected I was in for the empty paper bit, possibly even Act One, Scene One a few more times. If I'd known how many more—well I'm glad I didn't.

So it was decided for us to move to New York right away. After a day or two Rini got hold of a little place over on Central Park South with a bedroom so small you had to stick out your hand when you turned into the bathroom. No passing between the beds and the wall either—you had to walk across the beds if you wanted to go any place in that room. The living room was large enough for a small piano though, and the apartment was located at the back which made it completely great for concentrating because there was nothing to see out the window and no noise except at three o'clock in the morning when they picked up the cans, which operation would raise the dead.

Anyhow we moved in, got acquainted with the newsstand in the St. Moritz Hotel, the health store around the corner and the delicatessen in the middle of the block. Kermit wanted to set up another audition for a director right away. I tried making cuts in the meantime but we were still forty-five minutes too long when Rini and I went to Kermit's apartment one February night to audition for some "important people" Kermit said, "including Morton Da Costa."

# Chapter Seven

You'd think no audition would have been tough after that first night at Herb Greene's. How could there ever have been any more at stake than there was that night? Any audition should of been a breeze after that. But it doesn't work that way. Every audition is a world unto itself—microcosmic. And everyone in it is ditto. The afternoon of this particular one I even considered rehearsing with a real piece of cotton in my mouth—I swear the thought crossed my mind—to see if I couldn't get used to performing that way, just in case.

Kermit's big living room was crowded with people that night, practically none of whom I recognized. I asked not to be introduced to anyone individually till after I'd been on. Morton Da Costa was somewhere in that mob, I knew that. Also a couple other famous directors and set designers and even an angel or two—backers yet. And the all-important theatre men. Nowadays the Broadway theatres are so much in demand you have to audition for the theatre owners. If they don't like what they hear, you don't get a theatre. No Herb tonight. Wonder if Kermit would plant a few prop laughs among his friends. No, it never works.

Rini was putting a glass of water for me on the piano. A tall man with slightly gray hair walked in from the hall. He said, "Hello, Meredith. I'm sore at you." Hauling around from my preoccupation with myself I said "Thanks." When I forced myself to distribute his words into the proper slots he got my attention very easily. He was saying, "Every morning at eleven o'clock. Don't you understand? I was a 'listener dear.' Every morning at eleven I shaved while you gave me my Beethoven lesson on the radio. And what did you do? Took me up to Symphony Number Eight and cast me aside like an old glove."

"Well, the program folded," I says, preening and purring.

"That's no excuse," he said. "You should have continued anyway. Changed my whole life! Hell, I'm a damn longhair, and I wouldn't have been found dead with the stuff before." He started to sing, "Er-ohhhhica—Er-*ohhhh*ica." Kermit was trying to get my eye. I nodded happily and started toward the piano.

"See you later," I says, "Mr.—ah—"

"Shubert," he says, "John Shubert." Proprietor of the perfect theatre for *The Music Man*—the Majestic on 44th Street! The next thing I knew I was through the train scene and around the turn. Much obliged, John Shubert and you, too, Ludwig Beethoven.

Now I could settle back and enjoy this audition. The blobs in front of me began to turn into people. The tall angular man with the Slim Summerville look who doesn't

[ 86

smile would probably be Morton Da Costa. Well I'm not going to worry about him. He's probably just a deadpan. Or cultivates being one—considering he's such a famous director. Moss Hart wasn't any Andy Devine that night at Herb's, either. But then Mr. Hart wasn't enjoying it. Nuts. Okay, Morton Ichabod Da Costa, I'll play to the blond guy directly in front of me, enjoying himself like a completely relaxed friend of the family. He prob'ly *is* a friend of the family. Must remember to ask Kermit to invite this blond guy all the time. On the couch overt the right is a young kid, probably a teen-age friend of Johnny and David Bloomgarden. An Eagle Scout. Maybe a counselor. The extremely pleasant guy with the gray hair, God bless him, is my pal John Shubert, really laughing it up. If I hadn't met him earlier I'd have picked him for a set designer—maybe Jo Mielziner, or Howard Bay. They're supposed to be here tonight someplace.

Then Rini and I were into the reprise of "Till There Was You." In another four minutes I hollered "Curtain" and that was it.

Well, it was a big success—except for the one guy we wanted most to impress—Ned Sparks Da Costa. Not a smile, not a snick. In fact I don't believe he moved the whole evening.

I edged my way into the bedroom off the front hall to change into a dry shirt. Rini followed me in to give me a small rubdown and a big kiss. We had our foolish faces on good by the time we started back; and there he was. With his coat on and the door in his hand. Tall, wiry, inscrutable Mr. Da Costa. Looking me straight in the eye, this pipe cleaner in suspenders, this spawn of the great icecap, this William S. Hart in 3-D said, "Great. Best thing I've heard. Like very much to do it. Good night."

"Hey!" I says. Now I've never counted the words in the dictionary but I'm sure there's enough stuff in there from which to have made a better selection than *hey*—seeing as how I was going to use just the one word. I took a half nelson on myself and tried two more. I really came up with something fine this time. "That's *wonderful!*" I says. The man's back was being closed off by the door. "Hey, wait a minute! Mr. Da Costa!" He turned around.

"Bay," he says. "Howard Bay. Sets, lighting—all like that. I'm late. Good night." Howard Bay! Jeeminy crickets, just like that we got our set designer!

But where the Hell was Da Costa? Could be he wasn't here? As the young Eagle Scout counselor from the couch was leaving, Kermit grabs him and says, "Mere, here's Vince Donahue." Vincent Donahue. One of the top directors for stage and movies both.

"Enjoyed it," he says to me. "Quite a performance you and your wife put on, with all the characters the way you do."

"Thanks," I said.

Back in the living room I met Joe Anthony, director of *Most Happy Fella,* whom I'd picked for an investor; Bob Fosse, the choreographer, whom I'd picked for the elevator boy; Mrs. William Saroyan, whom I'd picked for Mrs. Bloomgarden's sister; G. M. Loeb, investor, whom I'd picked for an investor; and a dozen others. All this time Rini was talking with the pleasant blond guy friend of the family who had been such a great audience. They headed my way and I could see he already had his coat on.

"Congratulations," he said. I may not be able to get his next remarks down in the exact order but I'll vouch for the content, every word. I'll never forget them. "I don't know when I've heard anything fresher or more charming," he says. "Your lyrics are highly original and I love those excursions into dialogue in rhythm. What do you call those?"

"Speak-songs, I guess," I says. "Glad you liked them."

"Darling," Rini finally got her two cents in, "this is Morton Da Costa."

*"Hey,"* I says. "That's *wonderful!"*

We shook hands while I nodded my head very fast and very smilingly.

"I'll be seeing you," he says. "Very soon. Good night, Rini."

Another happy early-morning cab ride home. Howard Bay; The Majestic Theatre; and "Darling, maybe we've got Da Costa!" Rini had known who he was all along. She says, "I fell in love with his sensational head right away— and his big twinkly eyes and his smile and his freckles. Boy, that blond mane of his roars back on his head like a lion; a very nice lion." I says to Rini, "Do you know Da Costa's agent told Kermit he wasn't going to ask Da Costa to come tonight? Said he was already committed. Kermit says, 'Listen, let *him* decide if he wants to come or not. *You ask him!'* he says, 'if you want any more business with me.'"

Next day Mr. Da Costa repeated his enthusiasm for the show and his desire to direct it. "I'm still going to try to clear the other things," he says. "While we're waiting Meredith can pick my brains for a few weeks, if he'd like. I'd love to talk about the book. It's a little long." He made a slight side-to-side toss of his mane.

"How about the subplot?" Kermit says.

"I would think the spastic boy should go," he says.

"Meredith's working on that," says Kermit, "trying to sneak up on it instead of just tearing it out of there." Mr. Da Costa nodded, suggested ten o'clock the following morning for our next meeting. Da Costa meetings at ten? Bloomgarden meetings at nine? What happened to the all-night cigar-filled sessions ending up in aspiring chorus girls' bedrooms I heard about? When do they start getting temperamental? And demand that Rini stay away so as not to inhibit anybody's colorful vocabulary? Isn't everybody on Broadway supposed to talk in biological terms? Maybe that's not till the actual casting and rehearsals start. Those singers. And those dancers.

Mr. Da Costa lives on Central Park West. Rini and I were on Central Park South, some twenty-three or four blocks away. Not wanting to be late I arrived about fifteen minutes early, and not wanting to be early either I walked up to the Teddy Roosevelt Memorial and back a couple times, being apprehensive about would I be able to produce with a partner looking over my shoulder. I was uneasily afraid I wasn't the partner type. I tried to tell myself that even though Gallagher never spoke to Shean except on the stage, and Gilbert never spoke to Sullivan at all, and I was the son of my father who was Scotch, redheaded, and born in Iowa, there was always the possibility that someday the Winnebago River might run back up the hill around the bend away from the footbridge, the Senators might beat the Yankees, and I might be able to engage a complete stranger in a calm open-minded discussion preliminary to vivisecting my only child *his way.* I got to thinking about Ed White our butcher back in Mason City, how he used to illustrate the choice cuts on his own frame, widthing with thumb and forefinger a nice tenderloin along his side, chunking with both hands a fine rib roast, and outlining a shoulder of lamb as though he were installing the gold loops on the Admiral's aide at the Annapolis Graduation Ball. I admired once more, back over the years, Ed White's cleanish, reddish hands and the way he'd wrap up the quarter's worth of beefsteak, tearing off just enough butcher paper, unwinding string as needed from the cone atop the cash register, knotting it around the unmistakable little meat package and then, after two twists around his fingers, breaking off the cord with a grin and a sharp tug that ought to have taken the half of a finger off him but never did. Glancing up from those strong hands I looked into the fierce eyes of Colonel Teddy raring back on his horse. Now I was five minutes late and at the wrong end of my walk. I ran the six blocks to the Da Costa address, got my breath back on the elevator going up to the ninth floor and was admitted to the apartment through a large foyer, past a gold and white dining room into a huge living room decorated in European elegance providing a two-sided spectacular view of Central Park and the Fifty-ninth Street sky line. I had just taken note of a grand piano in the far corner, wondering how many times—and how soon—I'd be sitting over there demonstrating songs, when I heard "In here, Meredith. I'm in the office." Following the voice I got my first look at the dark red, wood and leather library where-in Mayor Shinn and his wife, the River City School Board, Tommy and Zaneeta, Marcellus Washburn, Mrs. Paroo and Winthrop, and all the other city-zians of my little north Iowa town would learn properly to behold-and re-act to-the unfolding in their midst of the love story of Marian, the Librarian, and Professor Harold Hill. Well, he called me "Meredith," so I waved my hand—a little unnecessarily, he being only three feet away—and I says "Hi, Tec."

Tec Da Costa started by asking for a complete new scene resumé. (I'll tell you about that name Tec. There are certain famous people in show business who have special names known to their friends. You have no stature at all in Hollywood, for instance, unless you refer to Loretta Young as Gretch, John Wayne as Duke, Cesar Romero as Butch, and George Burns as Nat. On Broadway, people try to impress you by working "Gadge" and "Tec" into the conversation as often as possible, those being the nicknames of Elia Kazan and Morton Da Costa respectively. "Tec," pronounced "Teak," comes from Tecoski, the original family name, and no one who really knows Morton Da Costa ever calls him anything but "Tec." Tec changed his name for professional reasons years ago making up "Da Costa" out of left field because it was easy and euphonious and was not too far from the original. Later, on his first trip to Europe, he made the amazing discovery that Tecoski wasn't the original at all. Some of Tec's ancestors had moved from Spain to Russia centuries before and had made up "Tecoski" as being more practical in their new homeland—also easy and euphonious and not too far from the original. You won't believe what they changed it from, but I'll tell you anyway: Da Costa. So when somebody says "Mort asked me to speak to you about an audition," or, "Morty said you'd ought to hear my voice," you know they're making it up.)

Well, we had just a fine morning. I never met anyone in the theatre less complicated, less frantic, or more artistically creative than Tec—or more coherent without being long-winded, or more communicative without being academic or vocabularically oppressive. Also, I never knew anyone at the top, in the theatre or out, who was so attentive to the ideas of the people he works with—so eager to weigh every possible alternative and suggestion. That first meeting was the beginning of a collaboration and friendship that never saw an angry word. (Except in California the first time he tried to drive to our Brentwood house from Warner Brothers. "You told me to turn right when you meant left."

"No, Tec, I meant right."

"I *turned* right and ended up at the Beverly Hills Hotel!" Oh those freckles were jumping that day.)

Tec followed me to the door as I was leaving suggesting that I come back as soon as possible with the new scene resumé as the best first step in trying to eliminate some of the tangent yarns we had agreed were cluttering up the main story. From that day I always walked home from our meetings, through the park, no matter what the weather—walking, as I may have mentioned, being the best stimulation, in my particular case, when I'm trying to turn things over in what I optimistically refer to as my think-tank. "Essays" for priming—walking for turning things over and selecting the best words for what you're primed to say.

James Agate, the great English critic, was asked a pretty ingenuous question once: "What standards do you apply to a play to decide if it's any good or not?" To this all-inclusive query the great man gave, not a stony silence, nor a two-volume treatise on dramatic criticism. He merely replied that in his view a play is good if he finds himself interested in what word the various players were going to utter next. Yes, the words, there's the rub, and the only way to get them is to hunt around for some good ones. Hunt for them in Central Park. That's as good as any place. Then go home and put them down on the paper. One after the other.

Within a couple weeks I had new stuff and old stuff all over the floor in our ten-by-fourteen back living room. One of those nights Kermit asked Rini and me over for dinner to meet his friend Billy Rose, not only a fine producer on his own hook but also by way of being a pretty fair journeyman song writer. After dinner Kermit asked Rini and me to do some of the score for Billy. We got off to kind of a bad start when Rini sang the love song and Billy says, "Let your husband sing it. I get thrown by your accent." Rini, having spent the greater part of her life in radio, concert and opera, took this as a reflection on her singing and was just about to leave him have one when I jumped in to explain on Billy's behalf, that we song writers prefer the lousy rendition of our fellows, where we can concentrate on the material, to a lovely vocal rendition by a professional singer. So I did ten or a dozen songs with just enough of the story to lead in to each one. Billy is a very warm audience when he's reached —reacts like a European—patted me enthusiastically on the head as he stood behind me there at the piano and even got to appreciate Rini's voice, accent or not, before he left.

"That's a great way to audition the show," Kermit says later. "We don't have to wait for you to get a new script down at all." In fact, he wanted to set up an audition right away the next night for some CBS people, mentioning that CBS financed *My Fair Lady*. Took the whole thing, he told me, somewhere around $300,000. One bite like that saves a lot of time running down individual financing. "Only three, four guys will be there," he says, "and you and Rini do just like you did here tonight for Billy."

"Great," I says, and gave it not a second thought.

The next night with my mind on a new scene I stepped out of the cab with Rini, in front of Kermit's apartment. I opened the door on forty, fifty people Kerm had run into during the day and invited up. The large couch was moved into the middle of the room for the four CBS guys. Tec was there also. That's what undermined my confidence, I guess. I wanted to have some real polished product before I showed off for Tec again. Can't let Kermit down, though, I thought, and now having planted that possibility, disaster was merely a matter of time. If you've really got so much Nero in you that you enjoy bloody details, ask Peter Witt the talent agent, or Hubbell Robinson, with CBS at that time, or one of the other CBS guys who were there, don't ask me. It was brutal. I just couldn't get on, that was all. Tried to ad-lib the story and got the last four drafts all mixed up. Tried to do the new piano-exercise scene I had just written and forgot the lyric. Tried to read it and couldn't find my place in the script. All in all I started over three times. And then quit. The silence was dreadful. Oh that silence. The only sound in the room was my dry upper lip refusing to slide down over my dry teeth. Normally I generate confidence in the train scene at the opening, knowing that if that should flop I have "Trouble" coming up. If that should miss, I still have "Seventy-Six Trombones" up my sleeve. Well, the great silence was never broken either by my pleasant ad-lib good evening joke, or by The Train, or "Trouble," or "Seventy-Six" by which time I was a broken-down derelict in a doorway, stuffed with cotton mather. The CBS people and most of the others left after a while. Very polite about it all. DOWN. DOWN. DOWN.

To my Bloomgarden memorabilia I add Kermit's remark as the limousine doors slammed in the driveway: "Good! Now I can get out the sturgeon. I didn't have enough to go around anyway."

Tec came up then and said to Kermit and Rini and me,

"I have managed to juggle my commitments around, I'm very happy to say. I'm free to do *The Music Man*. See you in the morning, Mere?" UP. UP. UP.

*Two* guys with the courage of their convictions; and we got them both.

# Chapter Eight

Well now. Morton Da Costa signed to direct, Howard Bay signed to do the sets and lighting, Raoul Pene du Bois to do costumes, the Shuberts have okayed The Majestic for us, and Kermit has selected December 19th for our New York opening. Our New York opening. Herb Greene and that downbeat. Glub! I never really believed it. Not even then. Clear up to the day. Couldn't hear that overture no matter how I tried.

I had finished writing the play again and started changing it again. At least I hadn't started with Act One, Scene One for quite a while, now. But I'd redo a weak scene, and that would upset a former scene— or a later one—and after while the cutting and pasting and arrows and signs made me start a whole new version anyway. I realize in reading over this account thus far, it sounds as though I had *planned* to write thirty or forty drafts, each one to be an improvement till the job was done —as you make a cigar, a wrapper at a time. Nothing could

have been further from my mind. I assure you that I
thought every draft I finished was a whole cigar. Every
one. And looking back through the stack now, which I
have only had the stomach to do once, I must say I can
see why I thought that. There's a lot of distillation in
there that I'm not ashamed of by a long shot. But handing
somebody a big fat script loaded with goodies, like the
trunk in the attic, is like handing them the dictionary, saying proudly, "It's all in there—just pick it out." A sculptor
is a guy who throws away rock, no question, no doubt.
But it took me a while to find that out.

New York's rain had now turned to snow. Franklin
Lacey had been in town for a week. We tramped through
Central Park, snow or no snow, usually going out at five
in the afternoon after I had communed with River City
by myself all day, trying to reconstruct the story line
without the spastic boy—I had decided he was doomed
and the time was now, and I had the kid narrowed down
to where I could see him replaced if I could find any
kind of related element to replace him with. It seems so
obvious now, to look back—like you'd like to run out into
that Central Park winter gloam and holler at those two
trudging guys, "Hey! You dopes, you. Look how simple
it is." Yeah, yeah.

Anyway, we made a date for breakfast the next morning
at Rumpelmayer's next to our apartment building. Franklin had to go back to California that night. Eating brioches
and croissants with the coffee the following morning I
found myself getting expansive on what makes a magic
moment in the theatre. Franklin was patiently listening.

"You don't know what makes it, you only know when you got it," I says. "I've seen *Fair Lady* three times and in that 'Rain in Spain' scene I don't think I'm hooked at all. I'm not interested except casually either in that flower girl or the professor. Hell's bells I know the story backwards and forwards till I'm numb from it—first I read it— then I saw the play—then the movie—now this *Fair Lady*. So I'm setting in the theatre each time being far from identified with the people up there and not giving a rap if the girl ever gets so she can say 'Rain in Spain' or not. You know the scene," I says. Franklin nods but I tell him anyway. "There's an indication of some hours of elapsed time. It's very very late. The other guy's asleep. Professor 'Iggins has his shirt loosened and his tie disheveled, and he is weary and bleary with fatigue, half asleep in his chair mumbling 'once more—the rain in Spain.' And the girl, who is hysterically weary herself, tries again without success. And then. And then. After a perfectly timed lull, she suddenly speaks in upper clahss Oxford English as follows: 'The rain in Spain lies mainly on the plain.' And every time she says it, when I'm in the theatre, I get goose pimples. Not just a reaction. Goose pimples. Big ones. And that is theatre magic. I can't even stave it off when I set there and know it's coming and try my darnedest to escape it."

"Theatre magic like that works best when you least suspect it," Franklin says.

"Sure it does, like in *The Music Man* when the school-board guys sing their first barbershop chord after hating each other for fifteen years. There's some more theatre magic in our show you don't expect, in the first-act finale where the Wells Fargo wagon is coming down the street and the townspeople are so eagerly waiting for it—the spot where the lisping kid comes out of the crowd so excited he busts out singing 'Oho the Wellth Fargo wagon ith a comin'.' Here's this kid who isn't even identified. Just a lisping kid but you get hit with some magic anyhow. Imagine if the lisping kid were somebody we know—some character in the story—then you'd have some real— What's the matter?"

Franklin was bug-eyed, grabbing the table with both hands. Then I knew what had hit him. It was spontaneous combustion. For the first time in his life—at least in my presence—Franklin whispered instead of hollered. The only reason I didn't drown him out was because I was doing it too. Together we whispered, "A lisping kid instead of a spastic boy!"

"Ashamed of his lisp—a big introvert problem child," I says.

Good-by spastic boy. I'll write a play about you some-day, if it's the last thing I do.

# Chapter Nine

I liked the new first act just fine except for not being quite sure about Marian's character dimensions yet. Also she needed a bigger song up front. Hell's Bells, I can take care of that out of town. Got to leave something to fix in Philadelphia. The new spastic-boy-less second act was still all over the floor. Hot or cold, however, Kermit, Herb and Charley Baker from the Morris office were coming over to our apartment the following afternoon to hear it. There hadn't been any talk about my needing a writer collaborator for a long time. I felt so good about the latest changes I began to think maybe there wouldn't have to be another writer. Writing into the last scene next day with my eye on the clock I remember telling Rini, "I *got* it. This time I *know.*" My poor darling Rini. Poor darling writers' wives every place. How often have they heard that before? It was half past one. The meeting was for two. I was in bed writing longhand. I hadn't shaved, bathed, or dressed.

[ 102

Rini answered the intermittently ringing doorbell as the different ones arrived. Once for Charley, once for Kermit, once for Herb. I kept writing. The bell rang again. Now who's that, I thought, just before I went into my last vacuum—coming down the stretch. After keeping them waiting, unavoidably, for about twenty minutes I finished and grabbed up the loose pages—the whole play was lay-ing on the bed—dashed into the living room in my pajamas and robe, and started, bang, with The Train. Rini tearing in from the kitchen just made it: "No it ain't, no it ain't, but you gotta know the territory!" Without stopping for any intermission we finished in about two hours, and there was the feeling. Nobody has to tell you when you get the feeling. "I told you I had it," I hollered at Rini who was sniffling a little because she felt it too. Kermit had on his special smile. "Very encouraging," he says. "Phone you from the office." Herb had been boffing me on, clear up to the tape. Charley had been with it, too. And also two guys I never saw before. They were introduced then though I was too excited to more than barely say Hodado, and we all rushed into playing the casting game, going through the whole circle of song-and-dance men again, which continued out in the hall and down the street after we said good-by. When they left, Rini and I were head-shaking again. Then I began to wonder who those two guys were.

It couldn't have been more than ten minutes later when Kermit phoned. "Mere," he says, "everybody loved it."

"Boy, I know I did," I says. "Who were those two guys?"

"Agents," says Kermit. "Baum and Newborn. They've been wanting to hear the book just in case."

"In what case?" I says.

"In case they could make a suggestion about casting."

"They handle writers?" I says.

"I guess they do. You don't need any writer. I can tell you now I haven't figured on any writer for months. I just met these two guys on the way over—"

"And you couldn't resist inviting them to the audition, I know, I know," I says happily.

With everything else tightening up as a result of the simplification of the subplot, Marian's lack of dimension loomed up big now—not just something you can plan to fix in Philadelphia. This girl's aloofness from her fellow townspeople, her failure to grab off a boy friend, her apparent snobbishness, remained unsatisfactorily explained. I had written pounds of description about her, and walked miles to try to find out for myself just what was the key to this girl's disposition. When am I going to learn that pounds don't help anybody but Tolstoy and James Joyce? I had to locate her in a phrase. Then let *her* take it from there.

And then, thank the Lord, to the sweet memories of those unexpected flashes of smiling fortune—the lisping-boy breakfast with Franklin at Rumpelmayer's; the sudden realization that "Trouble" would work without tune or rhyme; and that a train could be made up out of the sound of words—to those sweet trickles of juice from the grudging crabapple sack, I was able happily to add one short line of song-lyric that started the unraveling of the hitherto impenetrable cozy our Marian had concealed herself in.

Betty Hart from the Bloomgarden office had been spending days overt the apartment, not only helping me keep the physical work in order—drafts properly put together and taken apart, with the hours of typing, clipping, pasting and cutting attendant thereto, but also loaning me a finely tuned ear, this Betty Hart being a brilliant girl with a penetrating understanding of character dimensions and dramatic aspects thereof—in fact she is now head of Kermit's play and story department. Anyway, it was eight o'clock. We'd been at it all day. Rini and Betty had been sitting with their hats and coats on for an hour waiting to go to dinner. I was on the verge of preparing myself for the new, and, I prayed, final draft and was only putting off diving in till I could make some headway with Marian's character problem. Her first-act song—the first version of "My White Knight"—was at that time in the form of a short introspective ballad, expressing her longing for the guy of her dreams. When we know exactly what kind of guy that is, we ought to know what we don't know yet about this girl. Her lyric in this song, so far, didn't tell us enough. It isn't a Lancelot she wants, nor a John L. Sullivan. She's not a snob either—she doesn't want any egghead necessarily, nor is she afraid of getting a little manure on her front porch from the local Iowa farm boys. Okay, we know all that. What else? Maybe she just wants a guy who is not too Iowa-Stubborn to love her and to admit it once in a while. A guy who is not ashamed of the few nice

105 ]

things she likes around the house. Like the Marble Faun and Emerson's Essays. "A guy," I says, "who—for example —is not ashamed of a few nice things. Just someone who loves her, who is *not ashamed of a few nice things!*" And there it finally sat—just like that. Fell into the lyric like a clam in the chowder. And the three of us let out a holler and rushed out the door to dinner. One of these days I'd unravel Miss Marian for keeps. Now I knew.

# Chapter Ten

So it's June again—1957. Tec and Kermit had calmly put their chips on untried Onna White to do the choreography. Onna had been Michael Kidd's assistant but had never been on her own before. The Buffalo Bills barbershop quartette had been signed—theirs was the first *Music Man* contract. And rightly so. Look here. *There has never been a barbershop quartette in any Broadway show or in any motion picture. Ever. At no time. Except* The Music Man. No sir. Those familiar handlebar-mustache beer-barrel guys in the sleeve garters singing "A Bird in a Gilded Cage" with a tin-pan piano accompaniment like you saw in *Strawberry Blonde,* and *Meet Me in St. Louis,* and all the old tin-pan alley movies—those guys bear no relation whatsoever to any barbershop quartette. First of all, "Bird in a Gilded Cage" and "St. Louie" and all such ballads and one-in-a-bar waltz clogs like "Bicycle Built for Two" are not, never have been, and never will be any good for barbershop quartette singing. The harmony on the one

107 ]

hand presents insufficient challenge, and the tempo on the other is too unyielding for barbershop. And as far as a tin-pan piano accompaniment goes, no barbershopper would be found dead with accompaniment. Barbershop quartette singing, by the way, is the only art of its kind: where the pleasure is primarily for the singers—where performance for an audience is only secondary. Barbershoppers sing for *themselves* and for the pleasure they get out of an evening of "practicing," hunting for luscious chords and modulations—experimenting with this harmony and that. Strictly trial and error *faking*, which is something nobody learns. You have to be *born* a barbershopper. The requirements include a peculiar, particular kind of ear and soul for faking harmony. Symphony musicians can't necessarily do it, most opera stars can't do it. You mustn't be an individual when you sing—your voice has to be a straight-tone blending voice, not a soloistic, emotional, or trained voice of any kind. The lousiest barbershop quartette in the world, for example, would be Lauritz Melchior, Mario Lanza, Robert Merrill and Baccaloni. Also, the art of barbershop quartette singing is strictly an American one. You might even say it is the only true nonimitatable American music. Our Gershwin borrowed from Europe and was in turn borrowed *from;* our Charles Griffes, ditto; our Roy Harris, likewise; our Jazz greats, the same—today, there are as many great jazz players and composers of European background as American. But not barbershop. That's an American monopoly. And barbershop has never been on the Broadway stage. Except in the days of vaudeville: a good barbershop quartette always stopped the show with regularity no matter who else was on the bill. Oh the producers *thought* they were using barbershop quartettes in those Hollywood pictures, and in occasional Broadway shows. They sure weren't though. The amazing truth is that even today, in spite of the barbershop quartette societies that have contests monthly and annually and locally and regionally and every other way, to which people flock by the millions at a couple or three dollars a head (right in New York City, for instance, at Carnegie Hall, several times a year—and just try to get a ticket!)—in *spite* of all this the producers by and large, to say nothing of directors and agents, don't have any idea of what barbershop quartette singing is. That's why I put a barbershop quartette in *The Music Man*—and that's why those four guys stop the show in there, any time they want to—and *still* almost nobody in our business really understands the difference between a barbershop quartette and some other kind. You will only get redheaded as I do about the whole matter if you're a barbershopper, which thank the Lord, I happen to be. So, the next time you hear three, four or five, or ten guys over in the corner of the bar singing "Melancholy Baby," all carrying the air, including the guy with the low voice who, by singing the tune an octave lower thinks he's singing bass, and including your brother-in-law who does a high vibrant bulb-shattering imitation of Caruso, and including the waiter who plays a little banjo, *it's not barbershop.*

Anyway the Buffalo Bills were the first ones hired for *The Music Man*—poetically and rightfully so. Davey Burns had been spoken to for the Mayor. Barbara Cook, our unanimous choice for Marian, was definitely interested. Pert Kelton was a natural for Marian's mother, as was Iggie Wolfington for Marcellus, the professor's side-kick, or "actor's agent," as Cy Feuer would say. The star part was what was keeping us all awake nights. We went around the cycle again one afternoon overt the Imperial Theatre where we'd been auditioning a couple night club possibilities. As usual the suggestions came slower and slower and finally stopped altogether right back where we always started—with the forlorn hope: Danny Kaye.

"Fellas," says Herb Greene suddenly, "I got it." We sat up hopefully. "The only one to play this Harold Hill part is Ethel Merman." And if you think she couldn't, you're crazy. Then Tec says, "You know I think we're all wrong in restricting ourselves to song-and-dance men."

Kermit says, "You know, you're right? The part has developed in a different direction. This guy has got to be, first of all, a fine actor. Let's take our chances in being able to teach him to sing and move."

Well that really opened things up and the names flew thick and fast—Lloyd Bridges, Van Heflin, Art Carney, Jason Robards, Jr., Robert Preston, Laurence Olivier, Alec Guinness, Jimmy Whitmore, James Cagney, Andy Griffith. Planning to talk to certain of those guys, the meeting started breaking up. Rini and I were flying home that night and Rini hadn't finished packing. We had been away from home so long that Josephine and Piccolo and Cookie were threatening to join the army. Tec was walking up the aisle ahead of us. The house was dark except for the inevitable work light on the stage. Herb was still slumped in one aisle seat. Kermit with his lucky hat was just getting up opposite him—funny how the film always jams at those turning points to show you years later the detail of what happened, frame by frame. Tec said, "I think we ought to talk to Bob Preston about playing Harold."

"He took a few singing lessons off me a couple years ago," says Herb. "He didn't stay with it too long."

"I don't think we should leave out any possibility," says Kermit. "Let's look at him. Unless Mere gets Danny Kaye out in California. You know, everybody's taken a crack at him but you."

"Don't think I won't try hard," I says.

That was the last order of business before Rini and I embraced our partners "good-by" and went home to Josephine and Cookie and Piccolo.

# Chapter Eleven

Back in California I called Danny Kaye. Caught him in the M-G-M barbershop. He was affable and gay, addressed me after the manner of a fellow scissor-tail-coat batoneer, he having just come from Philadelphia where he had conducted Ormandy's immaculate Philadelphia Symphony in a Strauss Polka and the "Stars and Stripes Forever" in a benefit concert for the orchestra pension fund. I was eager to talk about *The Music Man* and this was my chance to get Danny to listen to "Trouble" at least, which I had rendered for Sylvia, Danny's wife, some weeks before in New York and which she had liked very much. UP. However I was too good an audience—not hard to be for Danny—and I could never get him down off the conductor bit long enough to get him interested in what *I* wanted to talk about. So I gave up and called Sylvia. She wasn't able to come to the phone so I left word. The whole day goes by and nothing. DOWN. Next day she calls. UP.

She says the part is not right for Danny and is pretty sharp with me when I argue. DOWN.

Next I had a talk with Dan Dailey's manager. Isn't it funny, I just happened to think how Dan and Danny have the same name, basically, but you could never switch their nicknames around—"Dan Kaye" and "Danny Dailey" would be ridiculous, like Arthur Carney and Art Toscanini, or Jack Gleason and Jackie Dempsey. Dan seemed like a perfect Harold Hill and we were dying to get to him. Dan's manager made a date with me for Dan to come over the following week to hear the show. UP. Our neighbors, Fred Zinnemann (the Oscar-winning director of *High Noon, From Here To Eternity, Oklahoma!, The Nun's Story*—isn't it nuts how you have to identify the great directors whereas everybody all over the world knows Jayne Mansfield?), and his wife Reneé came over together with the Martin Jurows to give us a little audience and some subtle support if and when needed—Fred, Reneé, the Jurows, Sterling Holloway and our preacher Mark Hogue were *The Music Man*'s first real friends, by the way—and there we sat. It was not only two o'clock the appointed time—it was 2:45 and then 3:15. I called Dan's manager and at length it developed that Dan had had to go to Phoenix to look at some horses, planning to return in a private plane to keep our date. As far as anything I ever learned subsequently, from either Dan or his manager, Dan is still there. DOWN.

The idea of Phil Harris, a few pounds lighter, had intrigued us in New York at one time. So I called Phil downt Palm Springs hoping to get him to listen to "Trouble." Got Alice on the phone and had a fine visit. UP. Phil was playing golf, would call me. UP. Nothing from Phil all day. Called Alice again. Fine visit. UP. Phil doesn't call. Speak to Phil's agent. Nothing. DOWN.

Get a very excited phone call from Herb Greene from New York. He had spoken with a mutual friend about Gene Kelly who was sure he would be interested. Herb knows Kelly quite well. Wouldn't he be great for the part? UP. Herb calls again the next day. He has reached Gene. UP. Not interested. DOWN.

That night I went to sleep thinking subconsciously about Danny Kaye conducting a Strauss Polka, and consciously how to make Marian's White Knight ballad into a big number in the first act. Since knowing she wanted a guy "who is not ashamed of a few nice things," the only thing that was holding me up was some kind of a rhythmic shove, I having already resolved to expand "White Knight" into one more nonrhyming tour de force, to balance Harold's big first act song "Trouble."

At about four A.M., my "sharp" period, I was wide awake going "d'dum-dum-*dum*, d'dum-dum-*dum*" in the polka rhythm of Danny, Strauss, and the Philadelphia Symphony that I had gone to sleep with. Rini felt I was awake and woke up, too. "Marian?" she says into the black, removing her earplugs. (Rini wears earplugs against the enthusiastic noises her husband makes on the frequent occasions he charges out to meet Morpheus a good deal more than halfway. She has developed some rare techniques in the use of these stoppers: One night when I was helping her to unwind by reading her to sleep out of the sport page I caught her with her plugs in. "Rini, how can you ask me to read you to sleep and then put plugs in your ears?" In order to ask this question I had to wake her up first and then wait for her to take out the earplugs.

"Very simple," she says. "I put the right plug only half-way in. I always start on my right side and when I drop off, the weight of my head pushes it in.")

"Yeah," I says. "Marian."

"All she wants is a *plain, honest man,* who is not ashamed of a few nice things."

"I know," I says. "D'-dum-dum-dum."

"All she wants is a *plain man,*" says Rini again. I jumped out of bed and grabbed my robe.

"A polka!" I says, "for this gal with her nice things and her Emerson Essays, and her Hawthorne's Marble Faun. Say what you said, Rini. Be Marian, be Marian!"

"All I want is a *plain man—*"

"—a modest man, a quiet man, with habits that do not exclude the occasional reading of a book!" I knocked it off and was back in bed in thirty minutes. Next morning it looked like this in the machine. *And it didn't rhyme.*

All I want is a plain man
A modest man, a quiet man
A straightforward and honest man, with habits that do not exclude the occasional reading of a book
I do not yearn for
Nor do I await
Any devastating, handsome, hand-kissing, wine-tasting silk pilla, hookah smoker
He need not necessarily be in uniform

I await no
Clean-cut, weather-beatened, square-rigged, white duck
pants in tennis shoes
No plumed hat, no splendid insignia
No Moose, Elk, Eagle, Odd Fellow
National Guardsman, Fire Chief, or Highlander
Be he from the Arabian Nights
Or the French Foreign Legion
No Lothario shoe salesman
No band leader
No railroad conductor
Or any other charmer
Either of me or anybody else
No Chautauqua Advance Agent
No vaudevillian
No depot telegrapher
I'm not dazzled over
Any such a kind of fascinating flame
All I want is a plain man
A modest man, a quiet man
A straight forward and honest man
To sit with me in a cottage somewhere in the state of Iowa
And listen with a smile
To a poem or a song
That is neither a five-line limerick about St. Peter and a man
from Duluth
Or a sing-song refrain of a purple cow
And not every day but just occasionally
We could walk down by the meadow
In the twilight-sprinkled dew
My White Knight
Can be blacksmith
Well-digger
Clerk or king
All I want is a plain man
A modest man, a quiet man
A straight forward and honest man

Whose habits do not necessarily include
The chewing of snuff
Or exploding root beer in the cellar every summer
And I would like him to be
More interested in me
Than he is in himself
And more interested in us
Than he is in me
And if occasionally he ponders
What makes Shakespeare and Beethoven great
Him I could love till I die.
Him I could love till I die.

And this new part then went right into "The White Knight" refrain:

My White Knight
Not a Lancelot
Nor an angel with wings
Just someone to love me
Who is not ashamed of a few nice things
My White Knight
Let me walk with him where the others ride by
Walk and love him till I die
Till I die.

Six years' labor on one lyric idea was done. I stuck it in an envelope to Kermit with a special-delivery stamp on it and carried it down the hill to the mailbox. The next afternoon he and Tec are on the phone from New York on the office extensions.

"Our girl has got some dimension now," Tec yelled, suddenly joining the hollerers' club. "I can't wait to hear the music."

"That makes two of us," I says.

"Didn't hear you."

"I'm not quite through with it," I says.

"You're on the right track, though!" Kermit says. I took a few more bows and hung up. The tune—this time I wanted a tune as well as an accompaniment—the tune not only dropped into place in a couple hours but did so with the kind of "inevitability" you always pray for, to where you could never bring yourself to change a note. I never have that rare experience with a tune without thinking of Oscar Hammerstein's plaint about the months he crawls up the wall for the words—compared to the effortless minutes in which Dick Rodgers knocks off the music.

Three days later I got a call from Tec, just arrived from New York—a whole vibrating receiverful of excited comments about the way Robert Preston had done "Trouble" for him in New York the day before. "Heard him with Herb just before I left for the Coast," he says. "Kermit is hearing him today."

"You talking about Robert Snowshoes Preston, half-brother of Chingachgook, and inventor of the igloo and the aluminum dogsled?" I says.

"I've got five words for you, Buster: wait—till—you—hear—him."

I had never met Bob Preston, never seen him even, except in those movies, and once on Broadway in a postwar drama called *The Hidden River* wherein he portrayed a phlegmatic young ex-army officer whose movement through the piece was required to be about as aerated as Sir Gawain in helmet and cast-iron pants dancing the

Minuet with Elsa Maxwell in a hoop skirt while accompanying himself on the contra bassoon.

"Hi," Robert Preston says forty-eight hours later as he precedes Kermit through our front door. "Bob is my name."

"Meredith," I says. "Never did figure out a very good nickname for that."

"Yeah. Meredith. That's a tough one. Wouldn't dare shorten that to Merde, now would we? No nickname, huh? Gotta work on that. Shall we get acquainted now or later?" Where were the snowshoes?

"Whatever you say," I says. He took off his coat, walked over to the piano. I gave Kermit a fast hello, hit an upper octave E-flat and Robert Preston disappeared into Harold Hill with

> Ya got trouble, friend,
> Right here—I say—
> Trouble right here in River City—

And that was it. (One of the greatest rewards of *The Music Man's* story is that it released Bob Preston from the wrong identity he had been strait-jacketed in throughout the greater part of his career. How this leprechaun of a volatile-witted seventh son of Thespis' most lighthearted and most happily gifted seventh sons could have been chained for so long in the ambling black-bear masquerade that not only obscured his true abilities but showed him, alas all too convincingly, in complete—and unfortunately, highly successful—juxtaposition to everything his great gifts clamored to really reveal—remains one of the fascinating mysteries in the world of the theatre. Watch him as

night after night he gives you an opening-night performance in the most glittering polish a role could ever hope to
receive. You have to watch closely to see those flashing
feet—yes the same *Northwest Passage* ones—as they seem
to touch the Majestic stage not more than twice in the
nearly two hours that Harold Hill is on view.)

# Chapter Twelve

Rini and I were chewing off our cuticle to get back to New York. Josephine and Piccolo were going with us this time, Rini having found a much roomier sublet down on 35th Street before we left New York. Josephine was elated to get away from the racket of some construction work going on in the neighborhood. (Why do they always do the jack-hammer drilling between seven and eight A.M., then tiptoe around like Minnie Mice the rest of the day? Josephine says, "Can't stand dot electric drizzle.") Poor Cookie had to go to Blackie's Cat Hotel. Blackie is a remarkable man who will not take your cat unless you agree to write to it every couple weeks. "Makes a difference," says Blackie, who takes your letter and opens it and hangs it in the cat's nighttime quarters to rub up against and smell of. The first time Rini wrote to Cookie was an experience, I may say. She sat at the desk looking at the paper for a while and then says, "Darling, I'm writing

Cookie and I don't know what to say." And you know I couldn't tell her?

Back in New York a succession of "firsts" started coming a mile a minute:

The first production meeting glistened with a special kind of professionalism I've never run into anywhere else but Broadway—the whole team together for the first time, Kermit and his staff, Morton Da Costa and his assistant Bob Merriman, Herb Greene, Onna White and her assistant Tommy Panko, Howard Bay, Raoul Pene du Bois, with Willa Kim and the Brooks Brothers representative, and Henri Caubisens, our stage manager. And Rini and me. Watching all that high-voltage so utterly organized was as beautiful a sight as I'll ever see. I know everybody else has said it but I have to say it too: here is where they separate the men from the boys.

(Is there a more beautiful sight in the world, be it an elevator starter, a viola player, a clamshell operator, a shoeshine boy, a sign painter, an architect, toastmaster, or Broadway producer, than a man who knows his business?)

It was also my first professional experience in a medium where the people pay to get in. And applaud only when they feel like it. The applause and laugh signs aren't any good on Broadway.

The "firsts" kept coming—made us almost ashamed to be so happy. The first sketches of the scenery—the big show curtain, The Train, the Wells Fargo Wagon, Main Street, the Library, the Gymnasium—all in sepia on huge sketch paper spread out on Kermit's desk one at a time by Howard Bay.

[ 122

The first album of costume sketches, the ladies' stately long dresses, huge flowered and feathered hats, the boys' knickerbocker suits, the girls' high shoes, the gym bloomers, 1912 nostalgia so beautifully colored and designed on the pages by Raoul Pene du Bois.

The first readings of scenes from the script by auditioning Marcelluses, Charley Cowells, Mrs. Shinns, Zaneetas, Tommys, Winthrops—although I must say you want to crawl in a hole the first time you hear some of your dialogue read up there on that stage. At least I did.

The first chorus auditions—the dancers and the singers. And at last:

FROM: Kermit Bloomgarden
1545 Broadway
New York 36, N.Y.     *THE MUSIC MAN*
Production Schedule

*Auditions:*
September 5th—Thursday. . . Open Call, DANCERS:
                     Women at 1:30 P.M.
                     at Imperial Theatre

September 6th, 7th and 8th. . . Open Call, SINGERS:
                     Women at 11 A.M.–
                     1:30 P.M.
                     at Imperial Theatre

September 9th—Monday. . . Equity Call, SINGERS:
                     Women at 9 A.M.
                     at Imperial Theatre

# Chapter Thirteen

The girls had been parading up there on the stage of the Imperial Theatre since nine A.M. They were being selected to play Wa Tan Ye girls—the young beauteous elements of our singing chorus—and had been chosen several days earlier in the week from auditions of groups of twenty—seen by Tec, then heard by Herb—there often being a hundred or more at a time backstage.

It was now five o'clock and the final choices had been narrowed down to those nine girls of whom eight were to be chosen. Tec, Kermit, Onna, Herb, Tommy Panko, Bob Merriman, Betty, Max, Vaughan, Rini and I were all clustered in the house about six rows back.

Herb was sitting in the aisle by this time—on the floor, in his favorite position: his legs crossed under him. Rini, who studies Vedanta occasionally, asked him, the first time she saw him sit that way, if the lotus position wasn't tiring and Herb said, "Not at all. My old man is a tailor and I always sit like this."

It had been quiet in the theatre all day; everybody was tense and concentrated, only we showed it while the girls remained calm, proud, poised and dignified. Tec had first selected them for type—young open Iowa faces, ingenuous, innocent, corn-fed; then for voice quality and musical ability; so it was now a final question of movement and attitude. Back and around and across went the nine finalists, across, around and back, now fast, now slow. Seven were just about decided on. We were finally down to picking the last girl out of the two that were left. Back and forth they went—all nine girls—all they knew was we only needed eight. Onna would suddenly ask for a change of pace, a particular kind of step—Tec would whisper something about complexion or style—Herb would remind us, in a hushed comment, something he had noted before about the relative quality of their high notes. And the nine walked around and across—over and back—heads up—eyes straight ahead. This girl was an understudy last year in a top company—that girl comes from Juilliard—that one had a concert career going till the magic of Broadway pulled her away.

Tec finally made his choice. He whispered to Kermit. Kermit whispered to Onna. They both agreed. Herb was satisfied. Rini and I, too. Tec signaled Henri Caubisens, waiting in the wings. Tec and Henri leaned toward each other across the pit. Henri nodded. And walked up to one of the girls. He said, "Janet, we'd like to have your phone and address please, in case we need a replacement at any time. Meanwhile thank you for being so patient and you may leave now."

"Thank you," she said, including us sitting there in the house with a partial turn of her head and a pleasant nod. Each of us murmured "Thank you" as she clicked off the stage still poised and assured—a Broadway professional from her pretty little blue silk shoes to her honey-colored, latest style hair-do. "Once more," said Tec to Onna. "Let's see the group all together one last time now." Onna called to the girls. Across, around, over and back they went—our final choices. "Let's hear them, Herb," says Tec. Herb cued his pianist in the pit with a Frank Loesser tune from *Guys and Dolls*. The girls picked it up like they were just starting out for an all-day picnic. Herb looked around grinning. The voices were great. But the second time around the whispering began again among us out in the house. Without the departed Janet something had happened to the balance—not their singing, the way they contrasted with each other. Tec signaled Henri again. Henri nodded. Then he spoke to the end girl, thanked her, and hurried off stage. We thanked her too from the house and Herb whispered to me, "She's got a job anyway. I would have had to take her out of *Most Happy Fella*." A minute of screaming silence dragged by. Henri, a little out of breath, now came back onto the stage with honey-blond Janet. There was no sign, no recognition from any of the other girls. At Onna's signal they went around the stage twice more. "That's it," Tec says suddenly. We all nodded and Tec walked down to the stage. "Girls," he says, "you have been marvelous through a very tough day. We're even worn out sitting out here so I know what you must be. Thank you from the bottom of my heart. The office will be in touch with you all." We started putting on our coats to leave adding murmured thank yous. The girls stood there. Kermit says, "Tec, they don't believe it."

Tec says, "I'm sorry, girls, I thought you understood me. You're *The Music Man* chorus. The office will be in touch with you about your contracts. You're engaged." Now they understood. Our poised young pros jumped three feet into the air, slapped each other's backs, screamed, laughed and hollered—none more so than three friends of Janet who now hysterically circled her. They had had to let her leave minutes ago without even a comforting wave. Watching the girls in amazement I poked Kermit. "Hey Kerm," I says, "they're all crying!"

Kermit laughed and says, "Yeah, I know," reaching for his handkerchief. Tec was too. And Onna. And Herb. And Rini. And Rini's husband. And Hank, the stage manager.

# Chapter Fourteen

The finals for the dancing corps were in the same pattern—heart-rending and heart-sending, simultaneously. Outside of a couple people like Gandhi and Albert Schweitzer, the truly professional Broadway dancer is the most dedicated human of our time. You appreciate this when you go through the birth process of a musical comedy. From the first rehearsal call to the opening-night curtain, the dancers never stop plying their craft—limbering, repeating classic steps, and practicing the new steps; limbering, classic steps, new steps, on and on as near to perpetual motion as you'll ever see the human mechanism get. Take five? Coffee break? Lunch? Not the dancers. The limbering, classic steps, new steps, go on endlessly. I never remember a dancer resting in a corner with a sandwich. Maybe around ten thirty at night you'll see a few, here and there; not lounging or sprawling with a newspaper, though—just out. Flattened. Collapsed. On top of a table. Or right there on the floor—the spirit still *plié*-ing, you may be sure, only the body had caved.

It would be seven days a week from here on in. No more free days for anybody. That's the way Broadway goes into the big push. It was mid-October. We would open in Philadelphia, November 18th. In New York—December 19th.

Rehearsals were set in a building of ballrooms and banquet halls down on 2nd Avenue—TV had long since taken over every playhouse, hotel, warehouse and loft anywhere around the theatre district. This rehearsal place was 111 2nd Avenue. I wouldn't have any trouble remembering 111. 111 Sutter was the address where I started my NBC radio career in San Francisco in the early 30's. Like everybody else in show business I'm a sucker for good-omen coincidences. I would be able to find my way down to 2nd Avenue without any trouble, too. I still carry a card in my pocket that sent me to the Bowery Winter Garden movie and vaudeville theatre for my first flute-playing job in New York—*August 26, 1919—Mr. Forman, leader—matinee 2 P.M.—Houston St. and 2nd Avenue—Don't forget to bring the piccolo.*

The company was complete now. All but Winthrop, the lisping boy. We had looked at nine million little Lord Fauntleroy professional stage kids and had no luck finding just an appealing natural-acting young one.

Rini let out a yell one night looking at TV. "There's Winthrop!" she says. I was leaning on the typewriter at the time and by the time I got to the end of the line or speech or whatever it was, I was too late. "He'll be on again next week," Rini says. "A little guy named Eddie Hodges, guessing songs on *Name that Tune*. He's Winthrop. Positively, exactly!" Rini was so determined about this kid she phones Tec and Kermit. The following week she hollers again at me. Again I'm writing, only this time Rini doesn't take any nonsense. She drags me to the TV. And there is Winthrop. I rushed to the phone to call Tec and Kermit. Tec was out, but Kermit said he'd turn on the show and call back. He didn't though because somebody phoned him about something else in the meantime so he missed the show, too. The next week Rini calls these two gentlemen the night before, the morning of, and at intervals, fifteen, ten and five minutes before the program— both Tec and Kermit. And they each catch the show. And they both phone back in great elation. Kermit says, "Rini you're *right!* You're *absolutely right!*"

Next morning the kid came to the Imperial Theatre, which we were still using for daytime auditions, and when he walked out on the stage we got hit with a dividend you couldn't have told about from black-and-white TV—carrot-red hair!

Winthrop has to play the cornet at the end of the show. Herb Greene immediately called a teacher for Eddie and explained we didn't have too much time. The teacher wasn't very encouraging about any ten-year-old kid learning the cornet all that fast, but Herb says, "I'll send him over anyway. Call me back after you talk to him."

The teacher calls back. "Mr. Greene," he says, "could I put a thousand dollars into the show?"

Eddie never needed but the one lesson on the cornet. (In fact the following year when he had to leave the company to make a movie for Frank Capra he says to Herb, "Don't bother getting a teacher for the new Winthrop, Mr. Greene. I can handle it." He did, too.)

Rereading this account thus far I note, among other things, that there are more pairs of parentheses in evidence than there are walking around backstage in Madison Square Garden at Rodeo time. Excuse me for one more pair, please, related to the subject of investing in the show, obliquely referred to above, but involving too many changes of tense to just continue on without some form of separation from the story. Also, set off like this, it's easier to skip if you want to. OPEN PARENTHESIS.

(On the subject of putting money into the show. I'd heard all about the eighty auditions Dick Rodgers and Oscar Hammerstein had to give before the money was raised to put on *Oklahoma!* And I was dreading when this phase of our Broadway adventure was going to rear its head up from behind the bedstead. I was constantly relieved on this score when it was pointed out to me that Kermit's reputation on Broadway with his record of hits—*Death of a Salesman, The Lark, Diary of Anne Frank, Most Happy Fella,* and seven or eight more—had given him a solid gold list of very satisfied customers and normally he had to fight them off with baseball bats. However, to cut legal expenses and delays in raising the money, Kermit had to restrict investors to New York State residents. This left out an appreciable part of Kermit's gilt-edged list residing in Connecticut and other states. And

131 ]

the business recession and shaky stock market at that time made the problem much more difficult. In fact these are some of the reasons why we did that rack-and-thumb-screw session for the CBS gentlemen. But Kermit never bothered me with money worries. Only three times did we actually audition for investors, and one of those times was for friends who had urged us to let them know about the show so they could let their friends in on it—and then they didn't come in.

How Kermit got the 300,000 simoleans I still don't know. I do know that Rini's and my good friend from NBC days, Ken Banghart, came in with a syndicate group he organized; so did Sylvia Drulie, an associate producer; and I found out later that Herb Greene raised $50,000 the hard way—a couple hundred, a hundred, even fifty, at a time—from friends and relatives.

"Papa," he said to his father, "I want your savings in this show and no questions asked." Herb's faith never wavered, starting with his first big boff laugh that sleety night in his apartment.

His relatives and friends are getting back ten for one these days, although Mr. Greene, père, still happily spends his days in the lotus position in his small tailor shop. His famous son often brings Broadway to his door, though. Once when Herb was coaching Rosalind Russell for a singing role they were on their way together to the rehearsal hall and happened to pass Mr. Greene's tailor shop. "Stop in to meet my papa for a second, Roz?" says Herb.

"Sure," says Roz. Well, Herb's father was as excited as

you would be if Rosalind Russell walked into your doorway. On his way home Herb stopped by again to find his father moaning with his head in his hands.

"Papa, what's the matter?" says Herb.

Holding up his right hand Herb's father cried, "All the time Miss Rosalind Russell was here I forgot to take off mine thimble!"

No, Kermit never bothered me with finance. He figured I had my own problems. That point I would never argue. And while we are so formidably parenthesized here, allow me to continue briefly with an answer to the next most-asked question: did I write a lot of songs I had to cut out and did I use a lot of stuff "out of the trunk"? I have yakked so much about the book itself, I haven't mentioned that its rewrites kept alternately demanding and eliminating songs. I should say two or three came from the trunk. All in all I wrote some forty songs, twenty-three of them between the opening of *The Silver Triangle* in Cy Feuer's apartment and the opening of *The Music Man* in the Shubert Theatre in Philadelphia. The final musical score as of the New York opening consists of eighteen not including the bits and pieces, and the ballets. Twenty-two numbers got cut, each one embracing the triumphs and disasters inescapable in the struggle for a beginning, middle and end, each song two small plays unto themselves—one entitled WORDS and the other MUSIC. Plus a three-page reprise for Mayor Shinn: "Ya Got Trouble, Mr. Hill," and a complete version of "Seventy-Six Trombones" with ancient instruments:

133 ]

There was a Pandean and a Picco Pipe
There were little Musettes and big Chalumeaus
There was even a Basset horn
And a long Cromorne
And a Tabor blown beneath the nose
There was an Aulus flute and a flute-à-bec
And a glittering Krummhorn wonderf'ly played
Then I casu'ly stepped inside
Of the only Ophicleide
Just in time to save the Big Parade

There was an Arghool reed and a Dulcian
There were quite a few Zinkens made out of wood
There were possibly three Schalmaeys
And a Cor Anglaise
And a Shawm which sounded awf'ly good
There was a Posthorn group and a Galoubet
There were several Waights and one crystal Nay
Then I spotted a Bombardon
Which of course I seized upon
Just in time, dear friends, to save the day.

Also a book of fifty-three experimental rhythm poems I had written trying to find ways of substituting rhythm for rhyme. The test was to add a musical accompaniment: with an accompaniment the "poems" should turn into satisfactory song—without accompaniment they should remain satisfactory dialogue. Try "Trouble," for instance, without any accompaniment, just reading it as plain dialogue. CLOSE PARENTHESIS.)

Well, the Bloomgarden office was now screaming for a final script. After half a dozen false starts I was finally out the door and down the street on my way to the Hart Steno Bureau with what I hoped and prayed was "It"

[ 134

when I remembered one last, last thing I had been putting off—Tommy, the juvenile's, surname. He had been just "Tommy" all this time. Passing a Sixth Avenue delicatessen that Rini and I were at home in, I found a mittel-European friend behind the counter. "Hi, Jan, are you Czech?" I says.

"No," he says. "Hi. I'm Bulgarian." And from him I got a brave last name for our good brave second-generation Tommy—the name of that superlative human being, that high ex-official in the Communist government in Yugoslavia who became disillusioned and wrote a complete exposé sitting right there in his homeland. The book was smuggled out, you will remember, but not that great man who, unbeknownst to himself, thus gave his name to a kid in a Broadway musical about Iowa—who would henceforth be known as Tommy Djilas.

So the final working script was put neatly between covers—a hundred copies of it. The final script. That was a pretty great day, too. The final script. Draft # Forty some-odd.

The actors were starting to memorize, rehearsal pianists engaged. Herb was elated—having just signed Larry Rosenthal, a great pianist-arranger, to work with Onna White in her creating of the choreography. And the days dwindled down nudging first the week, and then the day the company would all be together for the first time.

Tec had asked Rini and me to do our audition presentation of the show for the entire company on the first day of the rehearsal down there in the third-floor ballroom at

111 2nd Avenue. And the day did finally arrive. And there we were up there—really hamming it up, too.

After it was over everybody cried because Rini and I couldn't help playing the love scene pretty much for real. It took us just under two hours, skipping over the ballet numbers, of course. Tec says, "One hour for lunch." The dancers immediately went to work limbering and practicing.

At long last *The Music Man* was in rehearsal.

FROM: Kermit Bloomgarden
1545 Broadway
New York 36, N.Y.
JU 2-1690

*THE MUSIC MAN*
Production Schedule

*REHEARSAL SCHEDULE*

October 9th, Wednesday: Rini and Meredith Willson perform *The Music Man* for the entire company.
Time: 11 A.M.
111 2nd Ave.

October 9th, Wednesday: DANCERS ....... Time: 12 Noon
111 2nd Ave.

October 10th, Thursday and Daily: DANCERS. Time: 10 A.M.
111 2nd Ave.

October 10th, Thursday and Daily: SINGERS. Time: 10 A.M.
111 2nd Ave.

October 16th Wednesday: BOOK ........... Time: 10 A.M.
111 2nd Ave.

Daily Calls Until:

November 8th, Friday .................... Load out show.
November 10th, Sunday ............ Take in and hang show.
November 11th, Monday at 9 A.M. Orchestra rehearsal in Hall.
November 12th, Tuesday at 9 A.M. Orchestra rehearsal in Hall.

November 13th, Wednesday: Company en route to Philadelphia—9 A.M. train.
1 P.M. to 6 P.M. Orchestra rehearsal with cast in Hall.
Break two hours for dinner.
8 P.M.—Costume call at theatre in dressing rooms for entire company.

November 14th, Thursday: Technical rehearsal with entire Company and Orchestra.

November 15th, Friday: Afternoon: Technical rehearsal with piano.
Evening: Full Dress Rehearsal.

November 16th, Saturday: Afternoon: Rehearsal.
Evening: PREVIEW PERFORMANCE at 8:30 P.M.

November 17th, Sunday: Rehearsal to polish.

November 18th, Monday: Afternoon: Technical rehearsal to polish for opening
Evening: OPENING PERFORMANCE at Shubert, Philadelphia. 8 P.M. Curtain.

# Chapter Fifteen

We called our 2nd Avenue rehearsal hall Ratner's because one of the world's most famous dairy restaurants is Ratner's and it is located in this building. If longevity is related to what you eat, everybody should eat there because the waiters are mostly in the patriarch class and I'm sure they all eat on the job. You couldn't help it with all the gorgeous varieties of onion rolls staring you in the face from every corner of the table, and with the tureens of steaming soup passing by—hot borsch, cold borsch, lentil, noodle, vegetable, cabbage and half a dozen other varieties with egg, without egg, with sour cream, without sour cream. (I can't go further without telling you how to pronounce "*borsch*." Rini, having been born in Russia, taught me how to say it correctly. Most people say "borsht" with a big fat "t" on the end there. There's no "t" on the end or any other place. You should say—in two distinct syllables—"borsh-ch." That second syllable is pronounced just like it looks—just like you were going to say "chew," only you leave off the "ew" and just say "ch," which you can see does not even require the use of your vocal chords—it's all done in the mouth.) We all ate at Ratner's every day—the whole family of us. (Over sixty, we were, not counting the stage crew, which hadn't joined us yet. With the whole company intact I once made it out to be seventy-six, by a nice coincidence—counting Champ, our good kind gentle Wells Fargo Wagon horse who created the role and who never ad-libbed on stage until late in his first year in the part. Getting along, he was, and finally had to go out to pasture. Actually he was put to sleep shortly thereafter, which fact we had to conceal from the five kids in our company who were his dearest pals and vice versa.) The Ratner waiters were comforting—understanding of what actors go through at the formative phase of a Broadway show; in fact they became part of our family, too. One characteristic stands out in my memory. Never heard a Ratner waiter answer a question with anything but another question.

"Eli, could I have a couple eggs poached on a bagel?"

"If you could have eggs, why not on a bagel? Some law says you can't poach eggs on a bagel? Where? Where? Where is such a law written down?"

Forgetting yourself momentarily you might say, "And a couple strips of crisp bacon, Eli, please. With the poached eggs."

"Would never occur to you eggs with maybe a plate herring together? Salmon? Lox? White fish? Tuna? Shad roe? Caviar? You got to have bacon in a kosher dairy restaurant? You want also my head on the plate if I mention such a request in the kitchen? Or even here with other customers trying to eat in full view?"

The actors were getting their lines down now. Every day something new and exciting for Rini and me, like it was the first day in the world. Tec was calmly every place at once. Tec in a small banquet room setting up the book scenes—Tec in the ballroom setting up the production scenes; Tec with Herb in a lodge room down the hall hearing the singers, discussing movement and business and attitude. So many heart-stopping "firsts" during those Ratner days. The first time we heard our combined singers cut loose, for instance; the young Wa Tan Ye girls plus the Del Sarte ladies plus the "teen-age" River City boys plus the men. Herb called me in on the second day and knocked my hat off with that whole bunch belting "Iowa Stubborn," "Seventy-six Trombones," "Wells Fargo Wagon," and "Shipoopi," pretty well polished and nearly half-memorized already.

Watch Onna White for a while now—taking charge like a veteran her first time out on her own—no panic, no hysterics—thinking out steps and routines, with Larry Rosenthal creating the arrangements at the piano without a moment's hesitation, bar by bar. Can't do choreography any other way, you know. Can't write it down in advance— oh you can stay awake all night visualizing and planning, but the next day there in the hall you got to dream it up a bar at a time—and then go over it and over it hoping to the Lord that your kids will remember everything tomorrow you so painstakingly planned out today. And

Onna's kids always remembered and it was even tougher than that because Tec would come in every time he'd take a break from directing the book, suggest changes, new routines, and the whole tortuously erected structure would be torn down and rebuilt in the same bar-by-bar process, only now you had certain old steps to forget as well as new ones to remember.

Back in another hall Tec would map out the stage business he'd created the night before after rehearsal, every movement and every gesture had to be thought out—worked out—cross to the door on this word, look over your shoulder on that word, cross the girl on this sentence, she comes to you on that, all to be captured out of thin air and written down in Henri Caubisen's master script—much of it Tec would redo tomorrow replaced by something he liked better, brought out by the step-by-step process, word-by-word, action-by-action. And when Tec would say to a broad squatty farm lady in the Main Street scene, "What you're doing is very good for character, but with a different posture you might clarify the town's whole attitude toward Hill—like this," there he was in her place and somehow you didn't see Tec in his black slacks and rehearsal jacket, you saw a broad squatty farm lady leaning away from, yet into, an eloquent chip-on-the-shoulder arrogance that clearly and positively put this Harold Hill in his place. A moment later the "farm lady" disappeared to reappear opposite herself in some miraculous way in an imaginary green pinchback suit, button shoes and flat gray hat—Tec as an ingratiating irresistible Harold Hill.

As I remember, Tec spent two full days on the move-

ments of the River City-zians in the "Iowa Stubborn" opening that first week, yet it seems he must have spent fully
as much time on all the other production numbers, as well
as hour upon hour in the book scenes, working them out in
minute detail, not overlooking that people are people—
even dedicated ones—and if the director doesn't keep the
slack out of the reins the actors are going to continue reading their lines off the paper, for instance, instead of out
of their heads.

Well, two full days on "Iowa Stubborn" or not there
is nothing distorted about my memory with regard to
what happened at the end of that week, nine days to
be exact since our first rehearsal at Ratner's. On the tenth
morning at ten o'clock Tec got the whole company rounded
up from all the lodge halls, pantrys, banquet rooms, hall-
ways, loggias, and lobbies, and collecting everybody into
the main ballroom for the first time since Rini and I had
done our version for them, exactly—may I repeat—nine
days before. He said good morning and made the following
brief announcement. "Ladies and gentlemen, from the
top."

Two hours and forty-five minutes later *The Music Man*
had received its first performance from start to finish,
everyone doing his part ice cold. Which means from
memory. Which means by heart.

I hated every second away from 2nd Avenue but Rini
and I had to audition the show again—not once but three,
four times—for the record companies, which is what you
do when you have a forthcoming Broadway musical sched-

uled. The idea is that the original cast album of a Broadway musical is generally viewed as quite a plum for a record company. In order to show no favoritism you audition it for each, in turn, of the big four—Capitol, Victor, Decca and Columbia. Whichever company "bids" the highest, by way of guaranteed royalty, gets to make the album. I found this all out from Herb Eiseman, general manager of the Frank Loesser music company, which was publishing the score.

"Herb," I says to him, "I want to give the score to Capitol. I already played a couple of songs for Scotty out on the Coast and he flipped. They got a fine young progressive top-grade high-quality scrupulously honest company and why do we have to suffer auditioning the show for all those other people?"

That's when Herb Eiseman explained the routine you're expected to go through. "And besides," he says, "Capitol hasn't put in any bid yet."

Well, all full of confidence and borsh-ch I go to Victor's top brass to audition. Couldn't tear Rini away from Ratner's and it seemed like a capsule version of the show was all we'd been asked to present anyway, so I was doing it solo. The brass gathered, and I got on. I really did, too. I belted "Trouble" till you could hear me in Connecticut—nothing. Then "76"—nothing. Then "Till There Was You," "Wells Fargo," "Shipoopi"—nothing.

"Good-by," I says, "and thank you."

"Good-by," they says. "You're welcome."

Rini went with me to the Decca audition. Same deal. I mean the same thing happened only longer and more painful. I mean this time we did the *whole show* and got nothing. (In the silver-lining department there was that day—in addition to the top brass—a young guy and a young gal sitting in the back. We could see them reacting—although they had to hold in on account of not feeling like they should shatter the mortician atmosphere in the room. Rini and I played to them gratefully I may tell you. We didn't know how silver the lining, having no idea that Tom Prideaux was the young man—Entertainment Editor of *Life* magazine—and the young lady was Margaret Williams, one of his colleagues. Their enthusiasm that day developed into a six-page *Music Man* spread, and soon they would be working on that great U.S. Entertainment issue of *Life* for the following year which initiated the first double spread cover in *Life*'s history, a picture of one thousand and seventy-six trombones.)

The Columbia audition was nowhere near as painful—I mean we never did any. The brass over there sent word they had studied over the music and didn't need to hear the score.

And not one of the three companies put in a bid.

So when Scotty of Capitol called from the Coast registering considerable uneasiness about what was going on with respect to *The Music Man* cast album, Herb Eiseman thought it over for three, four seconds and said, "Scotty, you just got yourself a deal."

Next day Herb says "Mere, I got some good news. Our top man for records is Stu Ostrow. Says he knows you. He'd be the greatest man to handle *Music Man*. We've got a couple other new scores coming in and, of course, *Happy*

*Fella* and *Kismet* are still hot but Stu wants to go exclusively on *Music Man*." A score three record companies turned down, yet.

"Stu Ostrow?" I says. Sure. I remembered Stu Ostrow. Just a young guy. Back in '50 he came over to talk to me about Armed Forces Radio, my alma mater during the war. He was about to go into the Air Force to pay the government a couple years he owed them and hoped I could give him a recommendation to somebody in charge of the Entertainment part of the outfit, so he could keep progressing in music activity and theatre and like that if possible. I remember sending him to some colonel and getting a very nice telegram back from Stu thanking me. You often get requests like that but you don't often get thank-you telegrams back. Sure I remember Stu Ostrow and his telegram. I reproduce it here for a reason that will be clear to you later.

DEC 1951
DEAR MR. WILLSON THANK YOU FOR BEING SO KIND
I SHALL NOT SOON FORGET IT, RESPECTFULLY
STUART OSTROW A/1C USAF

# *Chapter Sixteen*

There were many more run-throughs down at Ratner's after that first week—maybe thirty-four, thirty-five. Everyone in the company reflected the calmness and gentleness of Tec—took on stature and pride at being the object of Kerm's creative generalship and Tec's brilliant sculpturing. Getting a show off the paper onto the stage requires constant tuggings and haulings. Not only dialogue rewrites, but the lyric and tunes undergo alteration too. It soon became evident, early and loudly, that the Buffalo Bills required another song in the second act.

When I write a new song I have to get out my walking shoes again. I was happier to be in New York for this purpose than home in California. A pedestrian out there is a misfit—a man in the wrong era—a spaceman in reverse—an odd ball. The dogs set up great hues and cries—children peer over hedges in alarm. After all there are no sidewalks out there. Using legs for walking is as archaic a maneuver as trying to wag your coccyx thinking it still to be a tail.

The cars fly by—the school buses soar past—and I cling to the thin air at the roadside. There's not even a curb —no lawn's edge—nothing—no lawn even. If there's any lawn it's in the back mostly dug out into a swimming pool with flagstone around. There's no porch any more on the front of the houses so why should there be a lawn in front? You don't pass the time of day any more with neighbors on the front porch or rocking on the lawn. Which is all right with me. Not that I don't miss that kind of friendliness but I have to think when I walk, which is why I'm walking.

So I started walking to try to get this new song going. I headed for Frank Loesser's. He lives on 88th and Park. I had a start by the time I got up there, went in and played it for Frank. On the way home I decided I didn't like it either and started a new one. A friend named Joe Dine has an office on the odd side of Park Avenue somewhere in the fifties. By the time I entered his neighborhood I had another song going pretty good. If I'd met Joe that day, we'd have visited at considerable length and I would have lost this new song probably, and the second act of *The Music Man* might have retained the song I was trying to replace on that walk—a song called "I've Already Started In To Try To Figure Out a Way To Go To Work To Try To Get You." The second act might never have recovered. Oh I saw you there, Joe, right in front of your office. If you noticed me cross the street that day I hope you'll understand—I had this song going. I was trying to get in an old-fashioned mood which required considerable concentration walking alongside Park Avenue's glass and aluminum skyscrapers. So I concentrated on Mama. If I can't get

Mama in the show any other way I'll get her in a song, I thought. Mama was preoccupied a great deal of the time with Ann Hathaway's life story. After Mama died I got to wondering about this. I can remember her often repeating her little Ann Hathaway joke: Ann sort of set her cap for Will Shakespeare, Mama used to say, and that she was successful, Mama said, could be attributed to the fact that "Ann Hath-a-way." That was the joke. And Mama quoted Ann Hathaway letters and had every kind of picture of Ann Hathaway's cottage and had made Ann Hathaway scrapbooks with every kind of clipping that ever mentioned Ann or her life or her family. So when Rini and I visited Stratford-on-Avon one time we were especially interested in Ann Hathaway's cottage with its thatched roof and its stiff-backed love seat where Will had sat trying to make time with Ann—or maybe vice-versa. Anyway we finally solved the mystery about why Mama was so interested in Ann. While walking through the cottage that day the guide said, "Ann Hathaway was seven years older than Shakespeare when they were married." I thought, That's a funny way to put it. She was not only seven years older when they were married but was seven years older before and after they were married and must have remained so till her death. Then I thought about Mama and all of a sudden I understood her interest in Ann Hathaway all her life. Very few of the kids of my generation, at least in my part of the world—if that has anything to do with it—ever knew how old their folks were, especially their mother, till after they had passed on. That day in Stratford I remembered how surprised we had been after Mama died to find out she was seven years older than my father. Lida, one of my mother's sisters, was older than her husband, too. I guess that was the girls' biggest secret. I had the new song finished by the time I got home. It was called "Lida Rose." Lida was Mama's favorite sister. Mama was Rose, short for Rosalie.

I carry a cane when I walk. It is made of yucca which is so light that it weighs practically nothing. Yucca is the California state flower and it is against the state law to ever pick the yucca blossoms or transplant the plants or cut the stalk. Still, I bought my yucca cane in a California store. I keep wondering about that.

The Bills sang "Lida Rose" the next day at rehearsal and liked it fine even though there had to be a little accompaniment in the second chorus because of the counterpoint song Marian was to sing simultaneously down the street on her front porch, a completely separate song called "Will I Ever Tell You?"

# Chapter Seventeen

It was like graduating day when we said good-by downt Ratner's. During the weeks spent in those banquet rooms everyone had found a little private cubbyhole for himself where you could stash your practice clothes, or umbrella or extra underwear. On that last day you loaded everything up on your script like it was your big flat geography book back in school days and then made the rounds for good-bys—exchanging tears and good lucks with the building manager and all their assistants, the superintendent, the elevator boys and the last and weepiest—the Ratner waiters.

"Eli, we'll celebrate *Music Man*'s first anniversary right here."

"So where else?"

(Barbara Cook's birthday a year later was celebrated with a big surprise party back at 111 2nd Avenue with happy memories at every turn of its unpredictable halls and stairways.)

The first uptown rehearsal was on the New Amsterdam Roof on 42nd Street, a real theatre, a real stage, instead of the marked-off unelevated areas in the large sprawling rooms we were used to downt Ratner's. The New Amsterdam was a jewel box of a theatre in its day, now shoddy and out of date but still encrusted with the glittering memories of Will Rogers, Fannie Brice, Eddie Cantor and Al Jolson. Here for the first time we saw our show in true theatre perspective.

After a few days' rehearsing at the New Amsterdam two hundred rubber-stamped slips were given out to the company. The slips were tickets to the first run-through for an audience, to take place two days later at two in the afternoon at the Barrymore Theatre on Forty-Sixth Street. Broadway.

Tec had saved the last hour before the run-through to polish up the march-on curtain call to the music of "76 Trombones." He always keeps a company occupied almost up to curtain time to keep them from worrying.

The hour slipped by. The march-on was ready. The doors were opened to the invited audience. Rini and I were excited, naturally. One more lovely "first." And if there are a few stoppings and startings, what's the difference? It's only for us and a couple hundred relatives of our company.

Only a couple hundred relatives? We could hardly get in the theatre. Broadway was there in force—producers, stars, directors, playwrights, composers, lyric writers, recording executives and music publishers. CBS guys, NBC guys, Agency guys. All there. Everywhere you looked was a household word and his brother. Rini and I sat next to Ginny Bloomgarden and you could of felt our three theatre seats pulsing with the slam-bang of our heartbeats. Rosalind Russell with her husband Freddie Brisson was in our row. Cy Feuer was just behind. Vincent Sardi, Greer Garson, Van Johnson, Harold Rome, Lawrence and Lee, Compton and Green, Paul Osborn, Frank Loesser, June Havoc, Robert Fryer, Andrew Wiswell.

Tec walked out from the wings and came downstage to big applause.

"This is our first run-through," he says as though he was merely saying "This is Thursday." He glances up at the balcony. "We have a few more in the audience than we expected." Two hundred slips and nine hundred showed up. "Without scenery it may be necessary for me to indicate the sets and the changes and the passings of time. We open in a red-plush railway coach. Meredith's play is set in the year 1912. The occupants of the railway coach are traveling salesmen, with one exception. You will recognize the exception when the time comes." Glancing at Herb in the orchestra pit about to conduct his "orchestra" consisting of one piano, Tec says, "I guess we're ready. We hope you will enjoy *The Music Man*, ladies and gentlemen." He smiles. "Please be kind," he says, and walks off. I breathe deep and grab for Rini. No orchestra, no scenery, no lights, no costumes. Just practice clothes, folding chairs for scenery, and a piano. Not even a curtain. And Broadway sitting there watching. Our salesmen come out and take the chairs representing the railway coach. "You can talk, you can talk, you can bicker, you can talk, you can talk, talk, talk, talk, bicker, bicker, bicker, you can talk all you wanna but it's different than it was."

"No it ain't, no it ain't, but you gotta know the territory!" I prayed for Herb Greene's boff laugh, but Herb was playing it straight. We're here to find out—let's find out. Somebody did laugh, however. Loud. And not solo, either. The reactions and laughs came fast and furious and kept on into the next scene. "Iowa Stubborn" worked big. Then came "Trouble." Bob Preston was electric. "Seventy-Six Trombones." And down came the bungalow. We can't believe any part of this. Rini looks at Ginny Bloomgarden who is learning forward, her mouth ecstatically open, her eyes wide and shining, her face wet with tears. Rini grabbed her arm. "Does it always happen like this?" she whispered. Ginny shook her head without taking her eyes off the stage.

"God, no," she says.

It went on like that in one beautiful crescendo. Intermission came and went, completely unrealized by us—Rini and I were afraid to leave our seats. The second act went just as big, mounting to a roar at the final curtain, which wasn't a curtain even, just Henri calling "Curtain!" And then he yelled, "Curtain up" for our first curtain call.

The piano started "Seventy-Six Trombones." Out came the dancers playing their pantomime trombones, swinging across that stage as proud as you'll ever wanta see anybody be. That's when the audience burst into spontaneous rhythmic applause as though cued to do so—as it has happened with every audience from that day forward. (Walter

Kerr described it a year later in a *Saturday Evening Post* article on the theatre, saying that "the rhythmic hand-clapping which greeted the finale of *The Music Man* on opening night was the only time I have ever felt a single irresistible impulse sweep over an entire audience and stir it to a demonstration that could not possibly have been inhibited.")

After the final "curtain call" I thought they were going to pull the theatre down. Andy Wiswell of Capitol Records was really enjoying himself amongst the recording fraternity. Rini and I were backed clear down to the orchestra pit and everywhere we looked people were laughing and crying and you couldn't hear yourself think. Who could think? Who wanted to think? Just stand there and breathe deep and be happy. Just let it all wash up there. Kermit forces his way through with his lucky hat on to hug us. "We're on the right track, Kerm," I hollers.

"You're *right*, you're absolutely *right*," he yells. Tec and Herb join us and we alternately babble at each other and shout across heads at this one and that one. Cy Feuer comes up. "Cut it to length, Mere, all you have to do!" he hollers. "Guaranteed hit! But don't use an orchestra."

"Why not?"

"It'll drown out the lyrics. You got a great lyric show here, got to hear every word! And don't let 'em speed up. With all those words you got in there it'll sound like Morse code."

We had to push our way backstage to congratulate Bob and Barbara and all the rest of our heroic family—flushed and dripping they were, all radiantly peering over the white fluffy edges of cloud 984.

And now I have to step away from that vibrating memory to answer a question, because so many people ask it I'm sure you're asking it too. After such an experience with such a demonstration by such a representative Broadway group, why any further apprehension about opening night? Are you not now positive sure you have a hit? No, reader dear. Listen to me, please. The answer is a big fat NO. Sentiment, emotion, fellow-show-people's sympathetic understanding, all these things can color a picture up pretty good. And the naked way you put on a run-through like that works tremendously in your favor. Many shows are even better that way where you imagine the big orchestra, the luscious costumes, the glorious sets. Some shows, extremely promising—even exciting in that "drawing-board" stage—never successfully withstand the opulence of production.

It started before we hit the street. As we left the stage door, which at the Barrymore is right next to the entrance, we saw him. He was holding court—high potentate of pessimistic prophecy. His familiar self-assured back, his slow side-to-side doom-dispensing head, the willing, eager manner in which his respectful circle of listeners was being oracled—even if you didn't recognize him, you knew here was a real Broadway Somebody. I didn't want to hear what he was saying. I wasn't ready to get kicked off our cloud yet. But some kind of Natural Law takes over in such a circumstance—capillarial, centrifugal, Newtonian, whatever it is, I heard what the man said: "They'll never

make it. Sympathetic audience like today is a pushover—
who doesn't love Preston and Cook in that crowd?" He
gets his fingers out ready to tick us into oblivion. "One—
where are the jokes? Two—the book is corny while the
lyrics are too smart. Sure they went over today with this
crowd but the public won't get it—won't want it—even if
they hear it, which they won't when there's an orchestra
in the pit. No dice, gentlemen, no dice. And I'll tell you
something else—" Well he didn't tell me anything else that
day. We went on down the street.

Next day the whispers grew and multiplied.

"Discount that terrific audience. That's not the guy who
pays eight-eighty, you know."

"Costumes, scenery, orchestration, all those things slow
a show way down as often as build it up."

"A lot of those people yesterday wanted you to fall on
your face, sure, that's par. But when the emotions start like
they did, right off the bat, they'll forget themselves and go
along with the poor bastards up there on that stage—they're
all show people under the skin."

"The people who buy tickets have gotta be shown. And
did you ever hear about critics? *They'll* tell you if your
show's any good."

The rehearsal schedule rolled along—nothing interrupted
it. Sometimes special activities were added, like Sunday
downt Brooks—the costume parade—another giant step in
the process of the characters coming off the paper. Mayor
Shinn's button shoes and square-cut coat; Zaneeta's red-
and-white Shipoopi dress; teen-agers in knickerbockers!

And the wigs—mountains of hair under the giant soaring hats setting like mother hens on the heads of the Pickalittle ladies; blond and brunet cascades tied with hair ribbons at the back of the Wa Tan Ye girls' necks. Virtue and racy imaginations meet head on in the leg-o'-mutton sleeves, the long skirts, the flowing hair, the petticoats, the hair ribbons, the high-button shoes.

Barbara Cook comes demurely onto the small costume platform—Marian, the Librarian, in a parade of her own— her severe little street suit and hat for her first-act entrance —her blue-and-white cotton, with hair ribbon to match, for the library scenes—her daffodil-yellow porch dress—her ice-cream-sociable dress with the big flowered hat dangling by its ribbon from her arm. Bob Preston in his white flannels, his pinchbacks, his extra waistcoats. Watch fobs, everywhere you look. Lodge pins and elks' teeth and gold chains and high collars, wide collars—stays—boas—plumes—sideburns—mustaches—every detail, checked and researched. This was Raoul du Bois's day—his first run-through—the first test of his dreaming, planning, researching, trial designs, final designs, executing—and now today the unveiling. Willa Kim was at his elbow, pins in her mouth, braces, gaiters and ribbons under her arm, pencils in her hair and a clip board in her hand, taking endless notes and changes. The hours melted and the company, laughing and talking excitedly, rushed back to rehearsal—nobody had to watch the call-back for them—who wanted an excuse to come late?—this was their show. Pros. Next stop—the Shubert Theatre in Philadelphia.

# Chapter Eighteen

The few days in Philadelphia preceding the opening included almost round-the-clock rehearsals. The company managed somehow to move into their hotel rooms and small apartments without missing a word or a note.

Rini and I checked in at the Warwick, dropped our baggage, and tore for the Shubert four blocks down the street. We couldn't find the stage door so we crashed the front of the house. Herb Greene was the first person we saw. Now Herb is a Broadway veteran of fourteen Broadway shows, but he was living today. "Hey Mere! Rini! Wait till you see what's on the stage—the Wells Fargo Wagon!" We went down the aisle, behind the left box, and saw our sets for the first time. The Billiard Parlor, the grocery store, the Gazette, the Bank, the filigree around the second story, the park, the hay in front of the Livery Stable, the locked rack around the Indian clubs in the gymnasium, Mrs. Paroo's porch light and the stained glass and that *stag* on top of the piano. Howard Bay hollers at us from the flies. "Go out in

[ 158

the house and we'll drop the Show Curtain for you." Down it comes. *Now* can you hear the overture? Look at the instruments. *Professor Harold Hill* in scroll letters at the top. They take it up again. Now we see the locomotive. Up it goes and there's the red-plush coach—every detail has come to pass, clear down to "an enamel drinking cup chained to the wall at the far end." We knew Howard's sketches and designs by heart but I must say we weren't prepared for the reality of the completed article, or the wallop and the lump that went with it.

Opening night galloped upon us. You talk to yourself a lot for that kind of occasion—keep yourself in check—never let yourself soar up to the "wouldn't it be great *if*" kind of speculation. There's so much precedent in show business for all your sparkling hopes to come whistling down to disaster in a matter of hours that you constantly talk to yourself to avoid it. The overture wouldn't be ready yet for a couple weeks. You throw something together for opening night. We had been at Herb's first orchestra rehearsal two days before and it was thrilling to hear the orchestrations the first time—but it was also a big jarring switch—there's a long way to go before the orchestra gets to be an old shoe like the nice unobtrusive rehearsal piano. Some of the stuff sounds good—some sounds horrible— numbers will have to be re-orchestrated—keys changed— routines shifted. And everything's too full—too loud. Everybody says don't forget you're liable to lose as much as you gain with the scenery and sets and costumes. Even the shoes get in the kids' way—new, tight-fitting and high— quite a lot different from their soft buddy-buddy rehearsal flats and slippers. The costumes will feel ponderous and clumsy and dripping hot. Think of all that broadcloth, all those petticoats and vests and hair—piles and mounds of long, coiled, hot hair through production number after production number—six, seven, eight, ten minutes at a stretch. Another thing. Those hair ribbons and high shoes and long skirts aren't what you call sexy-looking even if they do take you back to your early stirrings, as you might say, in high school days. You got to admit our kids looked a lot sexier in their scanty practice clothes at the Barrymore. And we know the first act is too long. A lot too long. And we know the acoustics in this huge house are far from perfect. This is a lyric show. If they can't hear it—they can't like it. The Barrymore was cozily intimate. The Shubert is a huge barn. So relax and take notes. That's why we're in Philadelphia. But still you sit in your seat with pounding heart and hope for a miracle.

Well, we didn't get one. Quite a few biggies in the profession were sprinkled through the theatre. At the intermission a famous lady producer who had hollered and cheered at the Barrymore run-through walked right by Rini and me at the end of the first act pretending not to see us. She wore on her face the unmistakable blend of relief and superiority characteristic of any producer who has the good fortune to attend another producer's fiasco. The lobby conversations I overheard were not very good and not very bad. Even at that, they liked it better than I did. Considering I had written the stuff and still couldn't hear three words out of four, I wondered why they were friendly at all. The second act is a complete blur in my memory. I

[ 160

took no notes after intermission, my tablet being already loaded down and spilling over onto my checkbook, my program and my soul. On the way to the box office to get my overcoat I saw him. Standing there. As usual four or five people were listening. He customarily looked at the floor as he gave his opinions. He did so now, shaking his head from side to side, slightly pushing his lips forward. "They'll never make it," he says. He had to come all the way from New York for the satisfaction of making that remark.

I get my coat. Rini and I meet Tec and Kermit going backstage where we kiss and hug our brave little army, hear a reassuring talk from Tec, check the call for the next morning and head for the hotel to try to unwind while waiting for the reviews in the morning papers at the same time—which can't be done.

"The magic is gone," Kermit finally says, voicing that awful realization that was crushing down on us all. The magic was gone and we knew it was gone. There were no two ways about it. I had tried to condition myself for anything—missed cues, noisy scenery, hung drops, wrong entrances, lighting mistakes, falling dancers, out-of-tune singing and holes in the dialogue. None of those things had happened. But the magic was gone. Everything we had been so excited about at the Barrymore was missing. I clung, now, to the fact that the lyrics weren't heard, trying to convince myself that was where the magic went. It was a lot more than that though. The whole look and feel was different. Had our imaginations supplied something that day at the Barrymore that doesn't exist?

At last the reviews came drifting in on hastily torn strips of that ugly whole-wheat copy paper, piecemeal at first, coming to life in small jerks, a spasm at a time—like those compacted little paper splinters you'd put into a saucer of water when you were a kid, that would tingle and shiver, if you waited long enough, and stretch out into Japanese water flowers that you could set there and really oh and ah about. And lo and behold, at two in the morning the completed pieces of those first official comments on *The Music Man* likewise developed into beautiful bouquets, full of charming detail and, for the most part, highly complimentary.

"Well!" I hollered out falling back on my chair in relief. "How do you do!" and different things like "great honk!" and "I'm a son-of-a-gun!" three, four times for each review. "If they like us this well opening night wait till we get the bugs out, hey? I guess we're in, hey? Kerm? We've all been too dang close to this show for too dang long . . . . . . I guess we're in, hey, Tec? . . . . . . Arthur, we're in, aren't we man?" Arthur Cantor, one of Broadway's great press agents, kind of grinned politely but didn't exactly look at me at the time. Nor did the others, exactly. Except for Rini echoing my ohs and ahs here and there, I guess I had been the only one to make any of these happy noises. Getting touched with a hot prickle of conspicuousness on the back of my neck I suddenly felt very first-of-May—like at the high school dance the first time I tried the one-step, when the floor was so highly waxed, and everybody was slipping and sliding all around but me because I had forgotten to take off my rubbers.

Oh everybody was pleased in an absent sort of way—a good review is a good review, a heck of a lot better than a bad review any way you look at it—Jeepers. But nobody's gloom, what you call, dried out.

Bob Preston came in. "Reviews are great, Bob," Kermit says.

"Yeah, I heard. Tec, the first act was very long where I was. How was it where you were?"

"Longer," says Tec.

"Look guys," I says giving up hard. "They liked it fine. These are high-class reviews—quality stuff, analytical—metropolitan as heck, and they liked it fine. It's all written down right there on the paper."

"Mere," says Tec. "Did you ever hear of Broadway?"

"Sure, but—"

"This is a Broadway show we have here, we hope. Regardless of how well they might like us here in Philadelphia or Washington or New Haven or London or Paris or Hong Kong or Gratz, it doesn't cut any ice. Remember *Plain and Fancy?* We murdered 'em out-of-town. Cheers—screams—bravos—the works, night after night and twice on Wednesdays and Saturdays. What happened in New York? Over fifty per cent of the critics hated it."

"Well, that's what I meant. At least you got **mixed** reviews."

"Oh come on, Mere. When more than half the critics pan you you're on such a ragged edge that it's just luck you didn't get one hundred per cent panned. I mean, there, but for some happy accidents like a balmy evening, a good

163 ]

meal, and a couple glasses of vintage wine, goes a unanimous full-blown turkey."

"Remember a show I produced one time called *Another Part of the Forest?*" says Kermit. "In Detroit we were sensational—in Wilmington we were the greatest—in Baltimore we were even greater—in New York we got killed."

"Meredith," says Bob, "we have just had one of those good nights that even a bad show can have. There are also bad nights that even a good show can have—which is more nearly normal. And we know we haven't even got a good show yet. Oh, these nice reviews will bring in the people and it is a lot tougher to whip a show into shape with empty houses, and the people will probably be receptive, but—"

"—but there's no rule about it," Arthur says. "Mere, did you know *Dark at the Top of the Stairs* is a smash in New York? It died here in Philadelphia only couple three, four weeks ago. Audiences can be tougher out-of-town just as well as they can be kinder and more sentimental. The point is you can't tell. We're trying to tell you to get realistic, Mere. You just don't count one single solitary chicken in advance in Show Business—not one."

"But the people in the theatre loved us tonight."

"Famous last words," says Kermit. "So they loved us in Philadelphia. If we were going to stay here a year—great."

"But we're not going to stay here," says Bob. "We're going to Broadway—one hundred and whatever-it-is miles northeast of here. And I'm going to bed and worry a little and then go to sleep because I know you and Tec and

Kermit and the rest of us are going to get the magic back into this show. Good night."

At three A.M. just before we all called it a day John Shubert telephoned Kermit. "Try to get hold of Ray Bolger," he says. "Only thing that will save your show."

Rini and I got in bed with our opening-night wires I had been carrying around since eight o'clock. The first one was from Stu Ostrow, my young friend of years ago, now at Frank Music who at his own request was going to be in charge of *Music Man* for record albums. I was thrown for a moment when I read an odd date down in the body of the message:

> NOV. 18, 1957     N.Y. TO PHILA., PA.   4:23 P.M.
> DEC 1951
> DEAR MR. WILLSON THANK YOU FOR BEING SO KIND.
> I SHALL NOT SOON FORGET IT. RESPECTFULLY
>                   STUART OSTROW . A/1C USAF

(He didn't forget, either. Besides the original cast album, twenty-one separate album interpretations have been recorded to date.)

The first thing I did next morning was to go to the theatre and investigate the sound system. I discovered that the center mikes in the footlight trough were deader than Kelcey's. No wonder I hadn't heard the lyrics. We got ahold of a sound expert in town. He looked things over and found only one speaker working. There were two—there should of been four—but the second was hung up backwards, its voice to the wall so to speak. Tec was unwinding miles of notes at a general session with the company. I had some other pretty good worries of my own, besides the bad sound. First of all there was something horribly wrong with The Train opening that would take more than an improved sound system to fix. Kermit had inaugurated a policy that no late-comers would be seated during The Train scene. But those in their seats that first night hadn't appreciated their chance to hear this spoken opening chorus undisturbed, and they read their programs as usual all through the exposition and everything else including the entrance of the star. All day I shook my head to myself about it, getting no place. That night I was standing in the back watching the show, too nervous to sit in a seat. The Train just laid there as before. Rini and I got lighted up at certain dialogue changes that strengthened the first act; UP; only to groan and moan at the weakening that somehow resulted way over in the second act some place. DOWN. And vice versa. (This happened almost every show one way or another the whole time we were in Philadelphia.)

The company rehearsed morning and afternoon the next day absorbing a dozen changes and refinements. I was an absent-minded ghost wandering through the theatre, chiefly account the ineffectuality of the dang Train. That night after the same thing happened again, our press agent, Arthur Cantor, nudged me and indicated the lobby. I followed him out where we could talk without disturbing the people in the back row. Milton Pollack, our company manager, was listening.

"Didn't you used to have the train start up?" Arthur says.

"That's the way I remember it," says Milton.

"Seems to me your train used to stand in the station, first time I heard it," Arthur says. "Then you had some dialogue in there that gave the effect of the train starting up and then getting faster, till she finally gets rolling. The way it is now, you go up on the train already moving. Maybe it doesn't give the audience a chance to quite get with it."

"We did it this way at the Barrymore run-through," I says. "Killed all the people. Anyway we can't start the train standing in the station. The great effect is when your show curtain goes up and you see the locomotive in full cry, steaming and snorting. When you burn through that scrim-locomotive and see the coach, how can you help but know the train's supposed to be moving?"

"I guess you're right," says Arthur. "I was just wondering."

"The one thing we *know* was different at the Barrymore was that we only had a piano accompaniment instead of an orchestra."

"So?"

"So tomorrow night," I says, "I'm going to ask Tec to try the train with just a piano or maybe without any orchestra at all. Everybody knows an orchestra can make a sound like a train. That's not news. Honegger did it, Villa Lobos did it, they do it in the movies all the time. The thing that hasn't been done is seven guys talking where their natural speech conveys the impression of a song and at the same time sounds like a train. That's news, as my friend Ernie Martin would say, and that is what has flown out the window on us and that is what we got to get back. Tomorrow, no orchestra in that scene. The following night we'll put back the drums with swatters. The next night we'll add some umpahs in the strings and so on till we hit the maximum amount of accompaniment we need."

The next night it was fifty per cent improved. So much so that we never put back any orchestra at all. No drums even. It was good, all right. But it wasn't *it*. We were amusing the people with it but we weren't killing them. Standing there in the back three, four nights later it suddenly hit me that we could have the train start up as Arthur suggested and still not have to change the effect of the shrieking locomotive tearing along as the curtain rises. As we bleed through the locomotive scrim to see the coach we can start *slowing down the train,* merely by slowing down the passing lights seen through the coach windows. I'll also scribble out a few bars for the orchestra with a few slowing-down grunts coming out of the tag end of the overture, which will bring the train to a complete stop. Then the conductor can come in announcing "River City Junction! River City, next station stop! All aboard!" Then I'll get out the old "starting-up" dialogue and start the train effect up from scratch with talk. Tec agreed we'd ought to try it.

Next day about three in the afternoon I brought in the new opening like this:

The train has come to a stop.

SALESMAN #1: Charley, your firm give credit?

CHARLEY: Naw, credit's old-fashioned.

(The lights now start to move back of the windows very slowly as the dialogue begins, also slowly, lights and talk gradually accelerating.) *Cash* for the merchandise, *Cash* for the buttonhooks—*Cash* for the cotton goods—*Cash* for the hard goods (gradually faster) *Cash* for the soft goods, *Cash* for the fancy goods, *Cash* for the noggins and the piggins and the firkins (faster) *Cash* for the hogshead, cask and demijohn. *Cash* for the crackers, and the pickles and the flypaper. (We're up to speed now.)

Look whadayatalk, whadayatalk, whadayatalk, whadayatalk, whadayatalk?

Wheredayagitit?

Whadayatalk?

And words, words, beautiful words, with the clicking "k's" and "ess aitches" and the sudden changes in inflection, would do the rest. Tec was excited about the way it looked on the paper. Setting there on chairs again on the empty stage the guys started to rehearse. Four or five times through and they were doing it from memory.

"Wait a minute," Tec calls from the house. "What does the overture do right at the very beginning of the scene?"

"Comes to a stop like a train does," I hollers, "just a couple slowing-down chords, like this: scrunch, scrunch—scrunch——scrunchchch—SCRUNCH. That's the train conductor's cue to come in with his 'River City Junction' line."

"Do that again," says Tec, "and when Mere hits that last SCRUNCH you guys jerk big in your seats." They did, enough to knock them loose from their teeth.

"That's it!" Tec says. "Now jiggle, in time with the words
—'whadayatalk, whadayatalk, whadayatalk,' everybody
jiggle, jiggle! You're on a rattle-bang passenger train approaching Meredith's home town!" Well it was just great.
Setting there watching, you had to jiggle yourself. And
nobody had to tell the guys to slow down at the end of the
dialogue and scrunch up against their seats in a neck-
breaking whiplash on Charley Cowell's final line "but he
doesn't know the territory!" SCRUNCH. And that train never
had to go to the roundhouse for repairs again.

The rehearsal went on to the next worry. I went on to
mine—the mystery of my pet, the "inevitable hunk"—"My
White Knight." Never had Barbara Cook failed to stop
rehearsals with that song. Never had she sung it downt
Ratner's without the rest of the company silently gather-
ing from all parts of the dang building to sit and listen and
cheer and applaud. Why wasn't it holding? For a couple
days we left it alone, just hoping the mysterious trouble
would go away.

Meanwhile, the Main Street scene was bogging down.
Too many jokes during the full-stage Main Street opening
chorus which follows. Tec cut down on the business, took
out three of five jokes, killed some business with the juvenile delinquent, painstakingly re-did some choreographic
movements cross by cross, step by step. "Mere," he says
one afternoon as he had maneuvered the River City-zians
all downstage to a final chord-finishing formation, "give
me sixteen additional full beats in the music and lyric for
this downstage movement. As a full chorus piece this scene

[ 170

ending doesn't take charge as it should for some reason."
I hurried back through the lobby to the ladies' toilet. Some
of our best stuff was written in the ladies' toilet—the only
place to concentrate in a theatre full of rehearsals. I came
back with a succession of town names set to music, names
very familiar in my beloved state. I sidestepped the temp-
tation to use some of the more colorful towns back home
like Correctionville, What-Cheer, and Diagonal, and stuck
to our metropolises: "Dubuque, Des Moines, Davenport,
Marshalltown, Keokuk, Mason City, Ames, Clear Lake."
It was better but we still weren't sure about this song
for such an important spot—the first true ensemble moment
in the show. Maybe it was too fancy. Somewhere along the
line the overlong first act maybe was suffering a little from
the need of a straight-forward melodic song, a more con-
ventional one-in-a-bar waltz, maybe, sung in rousing convincing unison. Maybe it should happen right there in the
beginning—early in the show. The only way you could tell
for sure was to try such a one-in-a-bar waltz opening. So
I disappeared into the Warwick Hotel to write one. Two
days later I came up with a new opening as follows.

> (MR. DJILAS sniggers loudly)
>      MARIAN (instinctively Madame Librarian)
> Did I hear laughing?
>      (Orchestra figure)
>      (TOMMY holds in as long as he
>      can and then bursts loose with
>      wild guffaws)
> I certainly did.
>   I heard laughing.
>   I heard laughing.

ALL

When there's laughin' at something that's funny
When there's smilin' at pleasures you've had
When there's goin' to bed with a dream in your head
And a kiss from your mom and your dad
When there's settin' and rockin' and thinkin'
When there's wishin' on stars in the sky
When there's Now and there's Then
And there's Someday and When
Not to mention the Sweet By and By
Who can cry about
Worries
Throw the varmits outside
Troubles
98% pride
Blessings
You've got more than your share
When you
Walk in the moonlight
Run in the meadow
And think about someone you love

When there's summer and winter and springtime
When there's cranberry time in the fall
When there's day after day of miraculous May
When there's nothin' to rile you at all
When there's bonfire time in October
With the punkins just bustin' with pie
When there's Christmas good cheer
And a Happy New Year
Not to mention the fourth of July
Who can cry about
Worries
Throw the varmits outside
Troubles
98% pride
Blessings

You've got more than your share
When you
Listen to crickets
Drink from a dipper
Chuckle a baby
And think about someone you love

MRS. PAROO

When your nose starts to run in November
With the promise of drippin' till May
When your groshery bill is as high as the hill
That your feet have to climb twice a day
When your temper is short and you holler
And your blood pressure only goes up
When you're full of bad news and your new button shoes
Make your bunion as sore as a pup
What's a couple more
Worries
Throw the varmits outside
Troubles
98% pride
Blessings
You've got more than your share when you
    (The NEIGHBORS have now rallied
    round and everyone comes up with
    a blessing)
Wash with soft water
Listen to church bells
Look at the sunset
Smell the white lilacs
Read Flip and Nemo
Pop Sunday popcorn
Make your own ice cream
Dibs on the dasher
Go on a picnic
Hear someone singing
Over the river

Wait for the twilight
Watch for the moonrise
And think about someone you love
Blessings upon you
All over and on you
With bushels and barrels of love.

I thought it was pretty good. Being eager to hear it I
bundled myself up in my eastern seaboard overcoat and lit
out for the theatre I had been away from the past two
days. I had dropped a couple pounds, I found out later,
which shows in my face when I'm that lucky. As I came
rushing into the theatre through the front of the house Bob
Preston was with Onna White in the middle of a new
routining of the Library Scene ballet. With one of his legs
up in the air he spotted me standing there in the darkened
house with a two-day beard, wild hair, and upturned coat
collar framing slightly sunken cheeks.

"Lazarus!" he cried. Well! I finally got me a nickname.
From that day Bob has never called me anything but Laz.

"Blessings" proved to everybody's satisfaction that the
song I already had, "Iowa Stubborn," was a very good
opening. I filed the two-day-old upstart away without a
backward glance. Tec had, in the meantime, got out the
old yellow legal-size tablet he likes to write on and had
cut and stitched and tugged at the first act's length and
proved we could close our third week with a pretty tight
show. One more week to go. Eight more performances.

Barbara Cook had proved something too, if it needed
proof—that she was a pro to end all pros. For three weeks

now I had experimented with the supposedly inviolate "White Knight." Each day, in the middle of everything else, I showed up with a new version of this song. A talking version. A cut version. A lengthened version. An inside-out version. An outside-in version. Why she didn't go berserk and stuff it down my throat I'll never know.

Finally, on Friday of the next-to-closing week, I got it through my thick head that, what with The Train, Iowa-Stubborn, Trouble, the Piano Exercise Song, Seventy-Six, and Pickalittle, we had enough specialties a'ready. By the time you get to Marian's big song late in the first act you better at least let her start with the feeling of a by-God ballad.

With a sad and reluctant pencil I deleted two "inevitable" pages of my favorite song, and reroutined the rest. When the moment came that night Barbara soared into the ballad chorus first. The audience was with her all the way. Including me—who got something else through my thick head that night. Standing in the back, I caught up with the true Marian—what she was—who she was. She was a certain girl graduate of the Armour Institute in Chicago circa 1880 who took her appreciation for a few nice things into a little Iowa town and spent her life scattering it among the kids in her Sunday school class, the kids in her kindergarten, and the kids just passing by the house; not to mention her own flute-playing slightly "abnormal" son. I had had Mama in the show all the time.

# Chapter Nineteen

Bob Preston never knew anything about his vocal chords—never knew he had any, as far as his ever having heard from them was concerned. He's a pretty good talker, too. Loves to talk about a role and the intricacies, gradations and subtleties lurking therein. I mean he likes to get unwound from a performance by sitting around later that same night talking about it, and how late he'll set there and talk depends upon how late you'll set there and listen. He doesn't exactly speak low, either—likes to talk up and be heard—a projector—a high-class hollerer, you could say. Throughout his acting career he has most certainly hollered his share of sides out over the footlights to the last row in the balcony, many roles from many plays, each of which you may be sure he has examined and analyzed out loud—and I mean pretty loud—after each performance down to the last pause, cross, eye-lift and behind-the-ear scratch in intense follow-through tones with all the take-charge and reach, vigor and earnestness of the actual performance itself. Yet he had never heard from his vocal chords in all that time. Didn't even know they go crosswise, not up and down, till Rini told him so one day while discussing singing and urging him to occasionally give his throat a rest. Well he finally heard from those chords—our next-to-last Saturday afternoon in Philadelphia halfway through the matinee. "You've never sung before," Rini had said a couple days before, "and you're therefore straining your voice because you're using it in an entirely different way than how you use it when speaking."

"Don't worry, Rinitchka," he had said. "My voice is made out of rawhide. It'll stand the gaff—always has." Then came this Saturday matinee. "Trouble" was already an effort. "76" was really forced. "Marian, the Librarian" was lost on the bottom and croaked on the top, and at the intermission Bob was a very bewildered, and practically *tacet*, actor. He bulldozed his way through the second act and that was all—there wasn't any more. Home to the hotel —bed—compresses—doctors—gargles—sprays. It happened so fast the whole company backstage and out front was shocked and bewildered.

Now if there was ever a lonely fellow, it is the star's understudy—while a show is being put into shape out of town. It's tough enough to keep the star abreast of the changes and re-routinings and new material let alone the understudy, who, therefore, entirely on his own, is desperately running from the fringe of one rehearsal to the tag-end of another, trying to keep up with the additions and cuts, and to learn the new business, dance steps and songs with no help at all from the director, the musical director or the choreographer. Our understudy was Larry Douglas, tall, slender, handsome, fresh from playing the lead in the touring company of *Pajama Game*. He heard Bob's performance that Saturday afternoon from the house, and by the time the final matinee curtain hit the stage he was into Professor Hill's first-scene costume. He had only three hours to rehearse the role and he wanted every second of it—one rehearsal—no orchestra, just piano —four production numbers in the first act alone—plus his song and dance with Marcellus—rhythmic walking business following Marian from scene to scene—vocal business with the school board quartette—the eight-minute ballet, which was also a song, in the library—to say nothing of the dialogue, forty-four minutes in one stretch in the first act without ever leaving the stage. Larry was still rehearsing when the overture began. No member of the company had eaten. No member of the company had left the theatre. Rini and I stood in the back. The overture hit exactly at 8:40 as the house lights went down.

Well, Larry went on. That night we had the great privilege of seeing the heart of Show Business and the pulse-beat that makes it life and death to those smitten with it— not the explanation as to why they go through what they go through to get to be part of it—I don't know any explanation for that—but the amazing raw revealment of what a real pro can do on a stage when he has to, and the strength that rises up in his fellow performers to carry him through. Every member of the company followed Larry's lines and lyrics along to himself in every scene, at

[ 178

the risk of going up, just to be ready to throw a word or cue. There were prompters in every portal—not only the stage managers but the light men, the stagehands and carpenters. The children were there, too, helping the prop men with Larry's props—the wig handlers and wardrobe ladies were up from the basement helping the dresser with his changes—no one getting in any one's way, a feat in itself, a big loving, zealous human machine taking care of one of its own, and when Larry came out for the final "76 Trombones" march-on the house exploded.

Bob stayed in bed till curtain time Monday. In his dressing room at half-hour he gave me a cautious "Hi Laz." Then he went over to his dressing table, grabbed one of those atomizer things, threw his head back and squirted his open mouth with a beautifully Mephistophelian gesture—the cape and sword-a-dangle stance. After that he brazenly looked me in the eye and went "Mi-mi-mi-mi!" Exit the actor—enter the actor-singer.

And enter our final week in Philadelphia.

# Chapter Twenty

The last week.

Five days.

Four days.

Three.

Two.

The company had been royally treated at the Variety Club every night of the Philadelphia stay. Now, coming into the stretch, a farewell Christmas party had been arranged for them besides. Everyone was there but Champ the horse. Bob Preston cut a giant surprise cake —trombones and cornets all over it. Benny Steinberg, Herb's assistant and concertmaster, found some chorus parts for the Hallelujah Chorus. Handing them out to everybody including Tec and Rini and me, and yes, Kermit, who had never sung a note of any kind in his entire life, we all got into the act for a wall-shattering finale to the *Music Man's* first Christmas party. The finale? Not quite.

Our kids had been swallowed up by so much mass adult participation they hadn't had a chance yet.

"Eddie," says Bob, "how about you and Marylyn doing something?"

"All right, sir," says Eddie Hodges, and he and ten-year-old Marylyn Siegel huddle in a corner like old troopers at the Lamb's Club planning a bit. "We're ready," Eddie says after a brief whispered conference with our orchestra pianist. Starting from the beginning of the second act footbridge scene Eddie and Marylyn did the complete love scene, dialogue and all, leading into "Till There Was You" which they sang just like Harold and Marian do it in the show including the two-part harmony and the big embrace at the end.

When Bob was able to talk he said, "You know something, kids? With you in it, this show just might run long enough for you two to take over the leads."

One day left.

Once Rini told me that two things impressed her more than anything else in her childhood. "Chocolate bars from Mr. Hoover, and my aunt's lorgnette." Passing a little gift shop near the hotel on the way to the theatre while Rini was in the room packing, I saw a lorgnette in the window. Gold with some small diamonds. The lady told me they came by it from somebody's estate. The diamonds on one side formed a crown near the engraved letters: *B. à J.* "Bonaparte to Josephine," says the lady. The other side had little diamonds forming a heart with an arrow going through: *J. to L.* was engraved here. "Diamond Jim Brady," says the lady, "to Lillian Russell."

"If you can get *M. to R.* on there by tomorrow morning," I says, "I'll take it."

So now I had the opening-night present. All that was missing was opening night.

We all stood in the back that last Saturday matinee—all but Herb, of course, who was in the pit and the actors who were on the stage—Kermit, Tec, Arthur, Howard, Onna, Raoul, Willa, Milton, Bob Merriman, Tommy Panko, Katherine Preston, Rini and I. A final rerouting in the library ballet seemed to work wonderfully. Everything else did, too. We looked at each other as the lights came up. "Freeze it?" asks Kermit.

"Freeze it," says Tec. "See you all in New York tomorrow." We embraced good-by in the lobby. Rini and I were driving back to New York the next morning. We hung around to wave good-by to our three busloads of family out on Broad Street. The scenery came hulking out of the alley. Champ sauntered down the street with his blanket and his trainer.

Well, one thing. We were satisfied we had done the best we could. The show was off the paper onto the stage according to all of our hopes and plans. We all agreed on what we had. Nobody said "If we only had one more week to re-do the second act," or write another song, or create another dance, or paint another set, or make some new costumes. Whatever it was, it was done the way we all wanted. Another week in Philadelphia? Or move on for a while to New Haven? No thank you. That's it. We hope they like it.

It is customary for the author of a new play to write something for the New York papers the Sunday before the Broadway opening. Next morning I read my last D-and-F-sharp type priming "essay" in the drama section of the Sunday New York *Herald Tribune.*

### IOWA STUBBORN

I lived in Mason City, Iowa, till I was sixteen. With my folks. My brother is a very smart man in the industrial field. Light aggregate concrete. In fact, he is an expert. I don't mind telling that to you, but it's the first time I've ever told it to him. That's what we call Iowa-stubborn.

My wife and I made a homecoming appearance at a home show in Des Moines seven or eight years ago and didn't receive enough applause to get us out onto the platform—there were a lot of Mason City people there, too, including several of my kissing relatives. That's what we call Iowa-contrary. ("Who do they think they are, anyway?")

In 1949 a couple people including Frank Loesser said, "I think you ought to write a musical comedy about Iowa." I thought it was a good idea and I wanted very much to do it but I refused, just to keep my neck bōwed.

Several others including my wife Rini had already made the same suggestion and I had already refused for the same reason. Nobody brought it up any more for some time, and I began to think they thought I couldn't do it. So, of course, I had to give it a try. That's what we call Iowa arrogance.

The existence of *The Music Man* proves Somerset Maugham's contention that anybody with a good memory can write down a story. I remember my childhood so well that each character in the show is not one, but a composite of three or four different people. One possible exception could be Marian Paroo (the leading lady, played by Barbara Cook) who is pretty exactly my mother, although I didn't realize this myself until the fourth week in Philadelphia.

Harold Hill (the starring role, played by Robert Preston) is so many people that I remember different ones every time I see the show. The period is 1912 when I was ten years old, so I suppose some of my points of view are reflected in the ten-year-old role of Winthrop played by Eddie Hodges. I'm pretty sure Mason City never had a mayor exactly like David Burns' Mayor Shinn, but the lady who used to help Mama clean house on Saturdays, a wonderful German lady named Mrs. Buehler, comes close to Pert Kelton's Mrs. Paroo, except that the German has become Irish.

Some Iowans who have seen *The Music Man* in rehearsal have called it an Iowan's attempt to pay tribute to his home state. I'm glad they feel that way because that's what I meant it to be even though I didn't try to rose-color up our Iowa-stubborn ways. Anyway, the show ("What there is of it and there's a lot of it, such as it is," sample comment from Cousin Phil) has been taken off the paper and put onto the stage with faithfulness. In taking pains and care in this regard it is Morton Da Costa's best, and although I haven't been on Broadway before, I've been around Broadway long enough to observe that Morton Da Costa's best is the best there is. The same goes for Kermit Bloomgarden and Herb Greene. And the company. And there goes my last alibi.

# *Chapter Twenty-One*

What a pleasure that gorgeous, sleek New York Majestic Theatre was after the overlarge Shubert in Philadelphia with the sound booby-traps. We had two benefits coming up—audiences who buy out the house for preview performances before the opening. This permits the company to get a couple shows under their belt—get used to the house and the new orchestra and the whole new feel.

Monday was rehearsal all day. On my way to the theatre I caught my breath to see a large red-and-white sign along Shubert Alley across from the Booth Theatre on Forty-Fifth Street. It was the first *Music Man* sign I'd seen in New York. I knew every crack and brick in that Shubert Alley—played the flute in the Shubert pit under Alfred Newman in 1927—did many's the dash for the stage door down that alley with only thirty seconds to make the overture—Down-Beat Willson they used to call me. On to Forty-Fourth Street to the Majestic—our new home—for how long, I wondered. I took the right turn across from

Sardi's—waved at Lou and Renée Shonceit in Mackey's Ticket Agency—passed the Broadhurst with its big AUNTIE MAME signs. And there we were. Huge blow-ups of photographed scenes from the show were all along the building.

Then I saw the marquee out in front of the Majestic, our theatre.

With the name there.

With the two l's.

Right up there.

I couldn't go in yet—had to call Rini overt the beauty parlor. She was just starting her manicure, she says. I says to drop everything and grab a cab and meet me at the Shubert Alley on Forty-Fourth Street. In ten minutes we took in that marquee together. It was really something.

The first benefit that night was fair—left us in a state of suspended animation, as you could say. The audience laughed in the right places and seemed to be as good as you could expect from a benefit audience, who, don't misunderstand me, are nice people and all, but the point is that (a) they all know each other so they're very late in their seats from yakking with each other in the lobby, and (b) they holler and whisper to each other a little during the show, and (c) they paid anywhere from five to twenty-five dollars extra for the tickets, so the "cause" can get a few bucks which is the idea of a benefit, but they are inclined to remember how much the tickets were and just kind of sit there and say "Go ahead, Buster. Make me react."

Tec called rehearsal for the following day, read quite

a few notes to the company, and started a complete run-through right from the top. That night—disaster. The second benefit audience was in character in spades. No laughs, no tears, very little applause, and very few reactions. The first act seemed to run forever and crushing, shattering catastrophe descended on us in the library ballet we all had thought was in such good shape which fell on its face—just laid there, making the first act about as lively as your High School valedictorian reading out loud from Bulwer-Lytton in Madison Square Garden without a microphone. Kermit and Tec met Rini and me in the lobby at intermission. We were trying to eavesdrop on the audience's remarks, yet also trying not to. Sure, our friend was there. The head-shaker. "They shouldn't have come in," he says to his little circle of calamity-phobes. "I mean they shoulda closed in Philly. Haven't got a chance."

Then, enter Brünnehilde—Onna White—from the other side of the lobby. Over to us she galloped, on a white charger, breastplate and sword and eyes all flashing—a Valkyrie on the loose with long golden hair flying out from her glittering helmet. This girl was really hit with something.

"I got it," she hollered. "Got it, got it, got it! I know, I know, I *know!* 'Marian, the Librarian' is a song, I don't care if the ballet lasts only thirty seconds with the dancers running around naked it'll seem too long unless Harold Hill comes back to finish off with the song he started with! Is that the way you wrote it in the first place, Mere, or isn't it?" My hurried nod wasn't necessary. "You're darn right," she says. "That's all that's the matter with that ballet, I know, I know, I *know!*" Believe me, when somebody *knows* like that, do what they say.

Tec made the change the next afternoon, the day of the opening. Another Valkyrie took on the colossal job of handwriting the entire music score and all the parts for that library scene—and with a smiling "no problem!" yet—Mathilda Pincus, the only woman music copyist in the business. Tec and Onna rehearsed the change till seven o'clock. It would have meant a major alteration for Bob any time, let alone the day of the opening. A tough switch. To say nothing of having to come back and nicely sing sixteen pay-off bars after dancing your head off for eight minutes. Try it, sometime. Not a gripe out of Bob, though. Not a murmur.

By this time Rini and I couldn't watch any more. Or stand. Or sit. Finally we went to see to the flowers and telegrams for our company. It was raining—good luck, they say. It rained on our wedding. Poured. I showed Rini the wire I had figured out for Kermit. WHAT BAND? it began, taking a Mayor Shinn line from the show. YOU ALWAYS KNEW THERE WAS A BAND, DIDN'T YOU KERMIT? Rini frowned.

"Aren't you asking for it a little there, my darling? Show people are pretty superstitious, you know. You're only supposed to say 'merde' and things like that, I think. 'Break your leg' and things like that." But I sent it anyway, Iowa-stubborn to the end, and then regretted it all the rest of the day. Rini went home to dress—called me back the minute she got there to read me a letter from Kermit he had left at the apartment with a beautiful opening-night present. I was in Milton Pollack's Majestic Theatre office at the time and this is what Rini read me over the phone.

"Dear Meredith and Rini, you have done a fine work, a glorious, happy show, and I am proud to have been associated with it. Whatever happens, meeting you and knowing you has made everything worthwhile. Love, Kermit."

Coming out of Milton's office I saw Kermit setting down in the lobby. It was about four-thirty. We could hear Tec and Onna and Bob rehearsing the library scene. Kermit had on his lucky hat, a little worse-looking even than normal account the rain. He hadn't shaved yet.

"Thanks for the swell present. And that letter," I says.

"Hi, Laz," he says. "You look a little down."

"You mean last night? Not at all," I says. "Jeepers, a dress rehearsal is supposed to be lousy, isn't it? That benefit last night was our dress rehearsal, wasn't it?"

"Sure," he says. "Anyway, in case you were down I could cheer you up. Last night, after the debacle, Max went over to Sardi's. There were some of the wrecking crew. Somebody said, 'Hi Max, understand you had a benefit preview at the Majestic tonight.' 'We did,' Max says. 'How'd it go?' somebody says. Max says, 'Lousy. We fell on our face!' 'Too bad,' they says. After a while a guy spoke up and says, 'You wanna know what I think?' Max says, 'Yeah.' The guy says, 'I think it's one of the great pieces of Americana. I was over there tonight. You can tell Kermit for me to save plenty of room on his trophy shelf for awards. He's gonna hit the jack pot with this show.'"

"No kidding!" I says. "Who was the guy?"

"Bill Saroyan," Kermit says.

We set there in the lobby for a while.

"See you tonight, Laz."

"You bet, Kerm."

Rini and I were setting in the farthest two seats overt the side under the box nearest the exit. Plenty places to hide, easy to duck out fast. I had a hold of her cold hand with its wet palm and she had my cold hand with its wet palm. Suddenly the show curtain got hit with a million candle power—and now, now, now, at long, long last, knowing positively it could never happen, Herb raised his baton. As it flashed down I imagined I could hear that big boff laugh of his in his apartment that cold rainy night one year ago to the day.

# Chapter Twenty-Two

A couple months after the New York opening Ernie Martin called me on the phone about something. "Hey Mere," he says, "I finally got to see your show."

"Welll How'd you like it?"

"You still haven't licked the book," he says.

MEREDITH WILLSON (1902–1984) was a musician, composer, songwriter, conductor, and playwright. Best known for the Broadway musicals *Meredith Willson's The Music Man* and *The Unsinkable Molly Brown,* he also wrote several autobiographical books, including *Eggs I Have Laid* and *And There I Stood with My Piccolo* (Minnesota, 2009).

MICHAEL FEINSTEIN is a Grammy-nominated entertainer and educator recognized as an expert on classic American popular music. He is the founder of the Great American Songbook Foundation and author of *The Gershwins and Me: A Personal History in Twelve Songs.* Learn more at MichaelFeinstein.com.